English	French
Here.	**Ici.** ēsē.
There.	**Là.** lä.
Over there.	**Là-bas.** lä-bä.
On/To the right.	**A droite.** ä drô·ät.
On/To the left.	**A gauche.** ä gōsh.
Straight ahead.	**Tout droit.** tōō drô·ä.
Do you have ...?	**Vous avez ...?** vōōzävā ...?
I would like ...	**Je voudrais ...** zhə vōōdre ...
How much does this cost?	**Combien ça coûte?** kôNbyeN sä kōōt?
Where is ...?	**Où est ...?** ōō e ...?
Where *is/are* there ...?	**Où est-ce qu'il y a ...?** ōō eskēlyä ...?
Today.	**Aujourd'hui.** ōzhōōrdvē.
Tomorrow.	**Demain.** dəmeN.
I don't want to.	**Je ne veux pas.** zhə nə vä pä.
I can't.	**Je ne peux pas.** zhə nə pä pä.
Just a minute, please.	**Un instant, s'il vous plaît.** eNeNstäN, sēl vōō plä.
Leave me alone!	**Laissez-moi tranquille!** lesä-mô·ä träNkēl!

Name
Nom
Home address
Adresse

Date of birth
Date de naissance

Address where you are staying
Adresse de vacances

ID/passport number
Numéro *de la carte d'identité/du passeport*

In case of emergency please contact
Personne(s) à prévenir en cas d'urgence

Important information (allergies, medicines, blood type etc.)
Indications importantes (allergies, médicaments, groupe sanguin, etc.)

In case of loss or theft, contact:
.... for traveler's checks
.... for credit cards

Langenscheidt

Universal-Phrasebook French

Edited by the
Langenscheidt Editorial Staff

Langenscheidt

New York · Berlin · Munich · Vienna · Zurich

Phonetic Transcriptions: The Glanze Intersound System
Illustrations: Kirill Chudinskiy

*Neither the presence nor the absence of a designation that
any entered word constitutes a trademark should be regarded
as affecting the legal status of any trademark.*

ISBN-978-1-58573-555-6
© 2006 Langenscheidt KG, Berlin and Munich
Printed in Germany

2. 3. 4. 5. 6.   11 10 09 08 07

4   FOOD AND DRINK

5   SIGHTSEEING

HOW TO FIND IT

This phrasebook contains all of the most important expressions and words you'll need for your trip. They have been divided up according to situation and organised into 10 chapters. The page borders have been colored to help you find things even more quickly.

Each chapter consists of example sentences and lists of words together with complementary vocabulary. This will help you put together exactly the right sentence you need for any situation. The easy-to-understand basic grammar section will give you further support.

Of course you can just show the person you're talking to the French translation of the sentence you wish to say. But the easily distinguished blue phonetic alphabet will enable you to speak your chosen phrase without any knowledge of French whatsoever. In order to give you an indication of the proper intonation, we have inserted punctuation marks into the phonetic spellings.

For vital situations we have also included sentences that go from French to English, so that a French person may also be able to communicate with you.

In order to cover as many different situations as possible we offer alternatives with many sentences; these are written in italics and separated by a slash:

Shall we get together *tomorrow*/*this evening*? **Si on se voyait *demain*/*ce soir*?**
sē ôN sə vô·äye *dəmeN*/*sə sô·ä*?

You can separate the alternatives into individual sentences, asking either

Shall we get together tomorrow?	**Si on se voyait demain?**
	sē ôN sə vô·āye dəmeN?

or

Shall we get together this evening?	**Si on se voyait ce soir?**
	sē ôN sə vô·āye sə sô·är?

When we offer more than two possibilities there will be an elipsis at that point in the sentence; the possible phrases to complete your sentence will be listed underneath:

I'd like a seat ...	**J'aimerais avoir une place ...**
	zhāmərе ävô·är ēn pläs ...

by the window.	**fenêtre.** fənet'rə.
in nonsmoking.	**non-fumeurs.** nôN-fēmär.
in smoking.	**fumeurs.** fēmär.

You can then put them together as needed, for example:

I'd like a seat in smoking.	**J'aimerais avoir une place fumeurs.**
	zhāmərе ävô·är ēn pläs fēmär.

Often you will also find sentence completions in parentheses. You can include these in your communication as you like.

Can you take me (a part of the way) there?	**Vous pouvez m'emmener (un bout de chemin)?** vōō pōōvā mämnā (eN bōōdshəmeN)?

If you wish to have someone take you the full way there, simply leave out **un bout de chemin**.

There are two equivalents in French of the English *you* (and *your*), depending on whether you are talking to a close friend or a child (in which case you say **tu**) or to someone you do not know or are merely acquainted with (where you use **vous**). We generally give the more formal **vous** form in the example sentences. Sometimes, however, particularly in the section on Human Relations, the differentiation can be very important. In such cases both forms are given, e.g.:

What's your name?   **Comment *vous appelez-vous*/*tu t'appelles?*** kômäN *vōōzäpḷä-vōō/t̲ē tāpeḷ?*

In French the form of the word used is sometimes dependent upon the gender of either the person speaking or the person addressed. In cases in which these forms make a difference to the pronunciation, we have indicated the different forms by the symbols ♂ (masculine) and ♀ (feminine):

I already have plans.   **Je suis déjà ♂ pris/♀ prise.** zhə svē däzhä ♂ prē/♀ prēz.

A man would say **Je suis déjà pris**; a woman would say **Je suis déjà prise**.

In French, nouns and their qualifying adjectives belong to either the masculine or feminine gender, and the articles differ accordingly. In cases where you can't identify the correct gender from the article (**l'** and **les**), we have used the abbreviations *m* for masculine and *f* for feminine words in the word lists. We have included the feminine endings with the adjectives only when they are irregular. You will find the rules for the regular endings in the basic grammar section of this book.

HOW DO YOU PRONOUNCE IT?

All words and phrases are accompanied by simplified pronunciation. The sound symbols you find in **Langenscheidt's Universal Phrasebooks** are the symbols you are familiar with from your high-school or college dictionaries of the *English* language.

For French, these basic symbols are supplemented mainly by ā, ē and N. These three sounds have no English equivalents and have to be learned by listening.

Vowels

Symbol	Approximate Sound	Examples
ä	The *a* of *father*.	**madame** mädäm **garage** gäräzh **tasse** täs
ā	The *a* of *fate* (but without the "upglide").	**été** ātā
ā	A sound that has to be learned by listening: round the lips for the *o* of *nose*; then, without moving the lips, try to pronounce the *a* of *fate*.	**deux** dā **œuf** āf **fleur** flār
e	The *e* of *met*.	**adresse** ädres
ē	The *e* of *he*.	**midi** mēdē **dire** dēr

12

Symbol	Approximate Sound	Examples
ē	A sound that has to be learned by listening. Round the lips for the *o* of *nose*; then, without moving the lips, try to pronounce the *e* of *he*.	**fumer** fēmā **le fumeur** lə fēmᾱr
ō	The *o* of *nose*, but without the "upglide".	**rideau** rēdō **rôle** rōl
ô	The *o* of *often*. In French, sometimes shorter, as in *moment*; sometimes longer, as in *sport*.	**moment** mômäN **sport** spôr
oo	The *u* of *rule*, but without the "upglide".	**trou** trōō **rouge** rōōzh
ə	The neutral sound (unstressed): the *a* of *ago* or the *u* of *focus*.	**je** zhə **demi** dəmē
N	This symbol does not stand for a sound but shows that the preceding vowel is nasal – is pronounced through nose and mouth at the same time. Nasal sounds have to be learned by listening.	**temps** täN **nom** nôN **matin** mäteN **parfum** pärfeN

13

Symbol	Approximate Sound	Examples
	Try not to use the *ng* of *sing* in their place.	

Consonants

Symbol	Approximate Sound	Examples
g	The *g* of *go*.	**gare** gär
l	The *l* of *love* (not of fall).	**voler** vôlā
ng	The *ng* of *sing*. (Occurs in some foreign words in French.)	**parking** pärkēng
r	The French "fricative" *r*. It is similar to the *j* of Spanish *Juan* and softer than the *ch* of Scottish *loch* or German *Bach*.	**rue** rē̄ **rire** rēr
s	The *s* of *sun* (not of *praise*).	**salle** säl **garçon** gärsôN
sh	The *sh* of *shine*.	**chapeau** shäpō
v	The *v* of *vat*.	**avant** äväN
y	The *y* of *year*.	**payer** pāyā **avion** ävyôN
z	The *z* of *zeal* or the *s* of *praise*.	**blouse** blōōz

14

Symbol	Approximate Sound	Examples
zh	The s of *measure* or the si of *vision*.	**jour** zhōōr **genou** zhənōō

The symbols b, d, f, k, m, n, p, and t are basically pronounced as in *boy, do, far, key, me, no, pin,* and *toy,* respectively.

The syllables of a French word are usually stressed evenly, with slightly more emphasis on the last syllable of a word or sentence. Therefore, stress is not indicated in this sound system – except in the following four situations in which the last syllable is not only stress-free but is barely pronounced as a syllable.

This absence of stress is shown through a preceding accent mark:

'ē: ē'ē   as in **fille** fē'ē

e'ē   as in **bouteille** bōōte'ē or **appareil** äpäre'ē

ä'ē   as in **paille** pä'ē

ā'ē   as in **feuille** fā'ē

ōō'ē   as in **grenouille** grənōō'ē.

'lə: b'lə   as in **table** täb'lə

k'lə   as in **siècle** syek'lə

g'lə   as in **triangle** trē-äNg'lə.

'rə   as in **libre** lēb'rə or **quatre** kät'rə or **descendre** dāsäNd'rə

n'yə   as in **ligne** lēn'yə or **campagne** käNpän'yə.

Combinations like the following are pronounced as a single "gliding" sound:

ô·ä   as in **roi** rô·ä or **voyage** vô·äyäzh

ô·eN	as in **loin** lô·eN
yeN	as in **bien** byeN
$\bar{\mathrm{e}}$·$\bar{\mathrm{e}}$	as in **nuit** n$\bar{\mathrm{e}}$·$\bar{\mathrm{e}}$ or **conduire** kôNd$\bar{\mathrm{e}}$·$\bar{\mathrm{e}}$r
$\overline{oo}$·$\bar{\mathrm{e}}$	as in **oui** $\overline{oo}$·$\bar{\mathrm{e}}$ or **weekend** $\overline{oo}$·$\bar{\mathrm{e}}$kend
$\overline{oo}$·e	as in **souhaiter** s$\overline{oo}$·et$\bar{\mathrm{a}}$

The final sound of a word is often linked with the initial sound of
the next: **il y a** $\bar{\mathrm{e}}$lyä, and a silent consonant may then become pronounced: **ils** $\bar{\mathrm{e}}$l + **on** ôN = $\bar{\mathrm{e}}$lzôN. This transition, called "liaison,"
is used quite frequently in French, but only the most important
and common cases are rendered in this phrasebook. (As you
progress in French, you will learn to use "liaison" with great
frequency.)

A raised dot separates two neighboring vowel symbols: **réalité**
rä·älēt$\bar{\mathrm{a}}$. This dot is merely a convenience to the eye; it does not
indicate a break in pronunciation.

Try to produce French sounds by speaking at the front of the
mouth, with vigorous movement of the lips, unlike English,
which is spoken in the back of the mouth, and with "lazy" lips.

Human Relations

HI AND BYE

Good morning.	**Bonjour!** bôNzhōōr!
Good afternoon.	**Bonjour!** bôNzhōōr!
Good evening.	**Bonjour!, Bonsoir!** bôNzhōōr!, bôNsô·är!
Good night.	**Bonsoir!** bôNsô·är!
Hello.	**Salut!** sälē!

INFO In France people say **bonjour** for "good morning" and "hello," as well as in the evening to greet someone, as with "good evening." One may also use **bonsoir** to greet someone very late in the evening; otherwise it is used to say goodbye to someone in the evening. **Bonsoir** is also used to say "good night"; **bonne nuit** is only used with children.

Do you mind if I sit here?	**Est-ce que je peux m'asseoir ici avec *vous/toi?*** eskə zhə pā mäsô·är ēsē ävek *vōō/tô·ä?*
I'm sorry, but I'm afraid this seat is taken.	**Non, malheureusement, c'est occupé.** nôN, mälərəsmäN, setôkēpā.
How are you?	***Comment allez-vous/Comment vas-tu?*** *kômäNtälävōō/kômäN vä-tē?*
I'm sorry, but I have to go now.	**Je suis désolé, mais je dois partir maintenant.** zhə svē dāzôlā, me zhə dô·ä pärtēr meNtnäN.

Good-bye.	**Au revoir!** ō rəvô·är!
See you *soon/tomorrow*.	**A bientôt/demain!** ä byeNtō/dəmeN!
Bye!	**Salut!** sàlē!
Nice to have met you.	**Je suis ♂ heureux/♀ heureuse d'avoir fait *votre/ta* connaissance.** zhə svē ♂ ārā/♀ ārāz dävô·är fe vôt′ rə/tä kônesäNs.
Thank you, I had a lovely evening.	**Merci pour cette charmante soirée.** mersē pōōr set shärmäNt sô·ärā.
Have a good trip.	**Bon voyage!** bôN vô·äyäzh!

SMALL TALK ...

... *about yourself and others*

| What's your name? | **Comment *vous appelez-vous/tu t'appelles*?** kômäN vōōzäplā-vōō/tē täpel? |

INFO In speaking to each other, the French use two different forms of "you" to distinguish between individual intimate friends and children – **tu** – and groups of people, lesser-known acquaintances, and strangers – **vous**. Use **vous** – the polite and plural form – for speaking with an adult outside of your family unless he/she indicates otherwise. Offering the use of first names is not an invitation to use the familiar form **tu**. Men are addressed simply as **Monsieur**, women as **Madame** or **Mademoiselle**, without the last name.

19

My name is ...	**Je m'appelle ...** zhə mäpel ...
Where are you from?	**D'où venez-vous/viens-tu?** dōō vənä-vōō/vyeN-fē?
I'm from ...	**Je viens de...** zhə vyeN də ...
Are you married?	**Est-ce que vous êtes/tu es marié?** eskə vōōzet/fē e märyā?
Do you have any children?	**Est-ce que vous avez/tu as des enfants?** eskə vōōzävä/fē ä dāzäNfäN?
Do you have any brothers or sisters?	**Est-ce que vous avez/tu as des frères et sœurs?** eskə vōōzävä/fē ä dā frer ā sēr?
I have a *sister/brother*.	**J'ai une sœur/un frère.** zhā ēn sēr/eN frer.
How old are you?	**Quel âge avez-vous/as-tu?** keläzh ävä-vōō/ä-fē?
I'm ... years old.	**J'ai ... ans.** zhā ... äN.
What is your line of work?	**Qu'est-ce que vous faites/tu fais comme travail?** keskə vōō fet/fē fe kôm trävä'ē?
I'm a(n) ...	**Je suis ...** zhə svē ...

Is this your first time here?	**C'est la première fois que *vous venez/tu viens*?** se lä prəmyer fô·ä kə vōō vənä/tͤ vyeN?
No, I was in France ... time(s) before.	**Non, c'est la ... fois que je viens en France.** nôN, se lä ... fô·ä kə zhə vyeN äNfräNs.
How long have you been here?	***Vous êtes/Tu es* là depuis combien de temps déjà?** vōōzät/tͤ e lä dəpē·ē kôNbyeN də täN dāzhä?
For ... *days/weeks* now.	**Depuis ... *jours/semaines*.** dəpē·ē ... zhōōr/səmen.
How much longer will you be staying?	***Vous restez/Tu restes* encore combien de temps ici?** vōō restā/tͤ rest äNkôr kôNbyeN də täN ēsē?
I'm leaving tomorrow.	**Je pars demain.** zhə pär dəmeN.
Another *week/two weeks*.	**Encore *une semaine/quinze jours*.** äNkôr ēn səmen/keNz zhōōr.
How do you like it here?	**Ça *vous/te* plaît ici?** sä vōō/tə ple ēsē?
I like it very much.	**Ça me plaît beaucoup.** sä mə ple bōkōō.
Have you seen ... yet?	**Est-ce que *vous avez/tu as* déjà vu ...?** eskə vōōzävā/tͤ ä däzhä vē ...?

Have you ever been to America?	***Vous êtes/Tu es*** **déjà allé aux États-Unis?** vōōzet/*tẽ* e dāzhā ālā ōzātäzẽ̄gnē?
You should visit me if you come to America some day.	**Si vous allez un jour aux États-Unis, venez donc me voir.** sē vōōzälä eN zhōōr ōzātäzẽ̄gnē, venä dôN me vô·är.
You're welcome to stay at my house.	**Tu peux coucher chez moi. Cela me ferait plaisir.** tẽ pä kōōshä shā mô·ä. selä me fere plezēr.
I'd be happy to show you the city.	**Je me ferai un plaisir de *vous/te* montrer la ville.** zhe me ferä eN plāzēr de *vōō/te* môNtrā lä vēl.

SOCIALIZING

Would you like to ...?

What are you doing tomorrow?	**Qu'est-ce que *vous faites/tu fais* demain?** keske *vōō* fet/*tẽ* fe demeN?
Shall we get together *tomorrow/this evening*?	**Si on se voyait *demain/ce soir*?** sē ôN se vô·āye *demeN/se* sô·är?
Yes, I'd like that.	**Avec plaisir.** ävek plāsēr.
I'm sorry, but I already have plans.	**Ce n'est malheureusement pas possible. Je suis déjà ♂ pris/♀ prise.** se ne mälāräzmäN pä pôsēb'le. zhe svē dāzhä ♂ prē/♀ prēz.

22

Would you like to join me for dinner this evening?	**Si on dînait ensemble ce soir?** sē ôN dēnā äNsäNb'lə sə sô·är?

➡ *Dining with Friends (p. 109), Going out in the Evening (p. 191)*

I'd like to invite you to ...	**Je voudrais vous inviter/t'inviter à ...** zhə vōōdre *vōōzeNvēta/teNvēta* ä ...
When/Where shall we meet?	**On se donne rendez-vous à quelle heure/où?** ôN sə dôn räNdāvōō ä kel*ar/ōō*?
Let's meet at ... o'clock.	**Disons qu'on se rencontre à ... heures.** dēzôN kôN sə räNkôNträ ... ār.
I'll pick you up at ... o'clock.	**Je passerai vous/te prendre à ... heures.** zhə päsrā *vōō/te* präNdrä ... ār.
Shall I see you again?	**On va se revoir?** ôN vä sə rəvô·är?

No, thanks

I already have plans.	**J'ai déjà quelque chose de prévu.** zhā däzhä kelkə shōz də prävē.
I'm waiting for someone.	**J'attends quelqu'un.** zhätäN kelkeN.
Leave me alone!	**Laissez-moi tranquille!** lesā-mô·ä träNkēl!
Get lost!	**Casse-toi!** käs-tô·ä!

COMMUNICATING

Does anyone here speak English?	**Il y a ici quelqu'un qui parle anglais?** ēlyä ēsē kelkeN kē pärl äNgle?	
? **Vous parlez français?** vōō pärlā fräNse?		Do you speak French?
Only a little.	**Un petit peu seulement.** eN pətē pā sālmäN.	
Please speak a little slower.	**Parlez plus lentement, s'il vous plaît.** pärlā plē läNtmäN, sēl vōō ple.	
? **Vous comprenez?/Tu comprends?** vōō kôNprənā/tē kôNpräN?		Do you understand?
I understand.	**J'ai compris.** zhā kôNprē.	
I didn't understand.	**Je n'ai pas compris.** zhə nā pä kôNprē.	
Would you please repeat that?	**Vous pourriez répéter, s'il vous plaît?** vōō pōōryā rāpātā, sēl vōō ple?	
What is this called in French?	**Comment ça s'appelle en français?** kômäN sä säpel äN fräNse?	
What does ... mean?	**Que signifie ...?** kə sēnyēfē ...?	

WHAT DO YOU THINK?

It *was/is* very nice here.	***C'était/C'est* très agréable ici.** sāte/se trezägrā·äb'lə ēsē.
Great!	**Très bien!** tre byeN!
Wonderful!	**Magnifique!** mänyēfēk!
Fantastic!	**Formidable!** fôrmēdäb'lə!
I like that.	**Ça me plaît.** sä mə ple.
With great pleasure.	**Très volontiers.** tre vôlôNtyā.
OK.	**O.K.** ōkā.
It's all the same to me.	**Ça m'est égal.** sä metägäl.
Whatever you like.	**Comme vous voulez.** kôm vōō vōōlā.
I don't know yet.	**Je ne sais pas encore.** zhə nə se päzäNkôr.
Maybe.	**Peut-être.** pətet'rə.
Probably.	**Probablement.** prôbäbləmäN.
Too bad!	**Dommage!** dômäzh!
I'm afraid that's impossible.	**Ce n'est malheureusement pas possible.** sə ne mäḻäṟäzmäN pä pôsēb'lə.
I'd rather ...	**J'aimerais mieux ...** zhemərе myä ...
I don't like that.	**Ça ne me plaît pas.** sä nə mə ple pä.

25

No.	**Non.** nôN.
Absolutely not.	**En aucun cas.** änōkeN kä.
No way!	**Pas question!** pä kestyôN!

BASIC PHRASES

Please; Thank you

Could you please help me?	**Est-ce que vous pourriez m'aider?** eskə vōō pōōryā mādā?

INFO In French, to reply "Yes, please" to an offer such as "Would you like another cup of coffee?," one would say **"Oui, merci."** or **"Oui, volontiers."** To answer a request such as "May I use your telephone?," say **"Oui, je vous en prie."**

Yes, please.	**Oui, volontiers.** ōō-ē, vôlôNtyā.
No, thank you.	**Non, merci.** nôN, mersē.
Thank you very much.	**Merci beaucoup.** mersē bōkōō.
That was very nice of you.	**C'était très aimable de votre part.** sāte trezemäb'lə də vôt'rə pär.
You're welcome.	**Je vous en prie.** zhə vōōzäN prē.
My pleasure.	**Il n'y a pas de quoi.** ēlnyä pä də kvä.
May I?	**Vous permettez?** vōō permetā?

I'm sorry.

Excuse me! **Excusez-moi/Excuse-moi!**
ekskēzā-mô-ä/ekskēs-mô-ä!

Sorry about that. **Je suis désolé.** zhə svē dāzôlā.

It was a misunder-
standing. **C'était un malentendu.**
sāteteN mäläNtäNdē.

Best wishes

Congratulations! **Meilleurs vœux!** meyār vē!

Happy birthday! **Joyeux anniversaire!**
zhô-äyā änēverser!

Get well soon! **Bon rétablissement!**
bôN rātäblēsmäN!

Good luck! **Bonne chance!** bôn shäNs!

Have a good trip! **Bon voyage!** bôN vô-äyäzh!

Have fun! **Amusez-vous bien!** ämēzā-vōō byeN!

Merry Christmas! **Joyeux Noël!** zhô-äyā nô-el!

Happy New Year! **Une bonne et heureuse année!**
ēn bôn ā ārāz änā!

27

FOR THE HANDICAPPED

I'm physically handicapped.

Je suis handicapé physique.
zhə svē äNdēkäpā fēsēk.

Could you please help me?

Vous pourriez m'aider, s'il vous plaît?
vōō pōōryā mādā, sēl vōō ple?

Do you have a wheel-chair for me?

Est-ce que vous avez un fauteuil roulant pour moi? eskə vōōzävā eN fōtā'ē rōōläN pōōr mô·á?

Where is the nearest elevator?

Où est l'ascenseur le plus proche?
ōō e läsäNsār lə plē prôsh?

Could you please take my luggage to the room?

Est-ce que vous pouvez transporter mes bagages dans ma chambre? eskə vōō pōōvā träNspôrtā mā bägäzh däN mä shäNb're?

Is it suitable for wheelchairs?

Est-ce que c'est aménagé pour recevoir les handicapés en fauteuil roulant? eskə setämānäzhā pōōr resevô·är läzäNdēkäpā äN fōtā'ē rōōläN?

Is there a ramp there for wheelchairs?

Est-ce qu'il y a une rampe pour les fauteuils roulants? eskēlyä ēn räNp pōōr lä fōtā'ē rōōläN?

Where is a restroom for handicapped?

Où sont les toilettes pour handicapés?
ōō sôN lā tô·älet pōōr äNdēkäpā?

I need someone to come with me.

J'ai besoin de quelqu'un qui m'accompagne. zhā bəzô·eN də kelkeN kē mäkôNpän'yə.

Human relations

address	**l'adresse** *f* lädres
alone	**seul** säl
to arrive	**arriver** ärēvā
boyfriend	**l'ami** *m* lämē
brother	**le frère** lə frer
child	**l'enfant** *m* läNfäN
city	**la ville** lä vēl
daughter	**la fille** lä fē´ē
father	**le père** lə per
friend *(male)*	**l'ami** *m* lämē
friend *(female)*	**l'amie** *f* lämē
girlfriend	**l'amie** *f* lämē
to go dancing	**aller danser** älā däNsā
to go out to eat	**aller manger** älā mäNzhā
academic high school	**le lycée** lə lēsā
husband	**le mari** lə märē
to invite	**inviter** eNvētā
job	**la profession** lä prôfesyôN
to leave	**partir** pärtēr
to like *(I would like to)*	**aimer** āmā
to like *(it appeals to me)*	**plaire** pler
to make a date	**se donner rendez-vous** sə dônā räNdävōō
married	**marié** märyā

to meet *(get to know)*	**faire la connaissance de** fer lä kônesäNs də
to meet up with someone	**se rencontrer** sə räNkôNträ
mother	**la mère** lä mer
no	**non** nôN
old	**âgé** äzhā
photograph	**la photo** lä fōtō
to repeat	**répéter** rāpātā
to return	**revenir** rəvnēr
school	**l'école** *f* lākôl
to see again	**revoir** rəvô·är
brothers and sisters	**les frères et sœurs** *m/pl* lā frer ā sār
sister	**la sœur** lä sār
son	**le fils** lə fēs
to speak	**parler** pärlā
student *(male)*	**l'étudiant** *m* lātēdyäN
student *(female)*	**l'étudiante** *f* lātēdyäNt
to study	**faire des études** fer dāzātēd
to take *(someone)* home	**raccompagner** räkôNpänyā
to understand	**comprendre** kôNpräNd'rə
vacation	**les vacances** *f/pl* lā väkäNs
to wait	**attendre** ätäNd'rə
wife	**la femme** lä fäm
to write down	**noter** nôtā
yes	**oui** ōō·ē

30

BUSINESS CONTACTS

On the Phone

➡ see also: Communicating (p. 24)

This is ... from ...

**Allô! Ici ♂ Monsieur/♀ Madame ...,
de la maison ...** älô! ēsē ♂ məsyā/
♀ mädäm ... də lä mesôN ...

I would like to speak
to ...

Je voudrais parler à ...
zhə vōōdre pärlä ä ...

! **Ne quittez pas.** nə kētā pä.
●

I'll connect you.

! **... est en ligne en ce moment.**
● ... etäN lēn'yə äN sə mômäN.

... is busy at the
moment.

! **... n'est pas là aujourd'hui.**
● ... ne pä lä ōzhōōrdvē.

... is not here today.

? **Désirez-vous laisser un
message?** dāzērā-vōō lāsā eN
mäsäzh?

Would you like to
leave a message?

At the Reception Desk

I'm here to see
Mr./Ms. ...

Je voudrais voir *Monsieur/Madame* ...
zhə vōōdre vô·är *məsyā/mädäm* ...

My name is ...

Je m'appelle ... zhə mäpel ...

I have an appointment
with ... at ... o'clock.

**J'ai un rendez-vous avec ..., à ...
heures.** zhā eN räNdāvōō ävek ..., ä ... ār.

31

! **Un instant, s'il vous plaît.**
eNeNstäN, sēl vōō ple.

One moment, please.

! **... arrive tout de suite.**
... ärēv tōōtsvēt.

... will be right here.

! **... est encore en conférence.**
... etäNkôr äN kôNfäräNs.

... is still in a meeting.

! **Si vous voulez bien venir avec moi.** sē vōō vōōlā byeN vənēr ävek mô·ä.

Would you come with me, please?

? **Veuillez patienter un instant, s'il vous plaît.** väyā päsyäNtā eNeNstäN, sēl vōō ple.

Would you please wait here a moment?

? **Est-ce que je peux vous apporter un café?** eske zhə pā vōōzäpôrtā eN käfā?

Would you like a coffee?

At Trade Fairs

I'm looking for the ... booth.

Je cherche le stand de l'entreprise ...
zhə shersh lə stäNd də läNtrəprēz ...

Do you have any information about ...?

Vous avez de la documentation sur ...?
vōōzävā də lä dôkēmäNtäsyôN sēr ...?

Do you also have pamphlets in English?

Vous avez aussi des prospectus en anglais? vōōzävā ôsē dā prôspektēs äNäNgle?

32

address	**l'adresse** *f* lädres
appointment	**le rendez-vous** lə räNdā-vōō
booth	**le stand** lə stäNd
brochures	**la documentation** lä dôkēmäNtäsyôN
building	**le bâtiment** lə bätēmäN
to call on the telephone	**téléphoner** tālāfônā
catalog	**le catalogue** lə kätälôg
convention	**le congrès** lə kôNgre
corporation	**le groupe industriel** lə grōōp eNdēstrē·el
conference	**la conférence** lä kôNfäräNs
– room	**la salle de conférence** lä säl də kôNfäräNs
copy	**la photocopie** lä fōtōkôpē
client	**le client** lə klē·äN
department	**le service** lə servēs
– head	**le chef de service** lə shef də servēs
documents	**les documents** *m/pl* lā dôkēmäN
earphones	**le casque** lə käsk
fax machine	**le téléfax** lə tālāfäks
hall *(auditorium)*	**le hall** lə äl
information	**l'information** *f* leNfôrmäsyôN
interpreter	**l'interprète** *m, f* leNterpret
management	**la direction** lä dēreksyôN
manager	**le gérant** lə zhäräN
to meet	**rencontrer** räNkôNtrā
meeting *(discussion)*	**la conférence** lä kôNfäräNs

33

meeting *(get-together)*	**la rencontre** lä räNkôNt'rə
news	**le message** lə mäsäzh
office	**le bureau** lə bẽrō
photocopier	**le photocopieur** lə fōtōkôpyẽr
price	**le prix** lə prē
– list	**la liste des prix** lä lēst dā prē
prospectus	**le prospectus** lə prôspektẽs
reception	**la réception** lä räsepsyôN
representative	**le représentant** lə rəpräzäNtäN
secretary	**la secrétaire** lä səkräter
session	**la séance** lä sā·äNs
speech	**l'exposé** *m* lekspōzā
telephone	**le téléphone** lə tālāfôn

Accommodations

INFORMATION

Where is the tourist information office?

Où se trouve l'office du tourisme?
ōō sə trōōv lôfēs dē tōōrēsm?

INFO The tourist information office (**office du tourisme**) will be happy to supply you with information about hotels, guest houses and rooms to rent in family homes.

Could you recommend a ...

Vous pourriez me recommander ...
vōō pōōryā rəkômäNdā ...

good hotel?

un bon hôtel? eN bônôtel?

inexpensive hotel?

un hôtel pas trop cher?
eNôtel pä trō sher?

boarding house?

une pension? ēn päNsyôn?

room at a private home?

une location chez l'habitant?
ēn lôkäsyôN shä läbētäN?

I'm looking for accommodation ...

Je cherche une chambre ...
zhə shersh ēn shäNb'rə ...

in a central location.

centrale. säNträl.

in a quiet location.

dans un cadre tranquille.
däNzeN käd'rə träNkēl.

at the beach.

sur la plage. sēr lä pläzh.

How much will it cost (approximately)?

Quel est le prix (à peu près)?
kel ā lə prē (ä pā pre)?

Can you make a reservation for me there?

Vous pourriez réserver pour moi?
vōō pōōryā rāzervā pōōr mô·ä?

36

Is there a *youth hostel/*	**Est-ce qu'il y a *une auberge de jeu-***
camping ground here?	***nesse/un terrain de camping* par ici?**
	eskēlyà ēn ôbärzh də zhānes/eN tereN
	də käNpēng pär ēsē?

| Is it far from here? | **C'est loin d'ici?** se lô·eN dēsē? |

How do I get there?	**Comment est-ce que je peux m'y**
	rendre? kômäN eskə zhə pē̄ mē
	räNd'rə?

| Could you draw me a | **Vous pourriez me dessiner le chemin?** |
| map? | vōō pōōryā mə dāsēnā lə shəmeN? |

HOTEL AND VACATION RENTAL

Hotel

Do you have a *double/*	**Vous auriez une chambre pour *deux***
single room avail-	***personnes/une personne* ...**
able ...	vōōzôryā ē̄n shäNb're pōōr dē̄
	persôn/ē̄n persôn ...

for *one night/*	**pour *une nuit/... nuits*?**
... nights?	pōōr ē̄n nē̄·ē/... nē̄·ē?
with a *full bath-*	**avec *bain/douche* et WC?**
room/shower and	ävek beN/dōōsh ā dōōblevā-sā?
toilet?	
with a balcony?	**avec balcon?** ävek bälkôN?

!	**Malheureusement, nous sommes complets.** mälärāzəmäN, nōō sôm kônple.	I'm sorry, but we're booked out.

I have a reservation. My name is ...	**On a retenu chez vous une chambre à mon nom. Je m'appelle ...** ônä rətənē shā vōō ēn shäNb'rə ä môN nôN. zhə mäpel ...
Here is my confirmation.	**Voici ma confirmation.** vô·äsē mä kôNfērmäsyôN.

INFO

Most double rooms in France have double beds. If you need separate beds, you must ask for **lits jumeaux** when reserving a double room.

The **cabinet de toilette** is a small chamber with a sink and sometimes a shower or toilet that is separated from the rest of the room by a wall. If the price of the room includes a **cabinet de toilette**, you should ask whether that includes a shower. The prices are always given by room.

How much will it cost ...	**Combien ça coûte ...** kôNbyeN sä kōōt ...
with/without breakfast?	***avec/sans* le petit déjeuner?** ävek/säN lə pətē dāzhānā?
with *half/full* board?	**avec la *demi-pension/pension complète*?** ävek lä dəmēpäNsyôN/päNsyôN kôNplet?
May I have a look at the room?	**Je pourrais voir la chambre?** zhə pōōre vô·är lä shäNb'rə?

| Do you have a ... room? | **Vous auriez encore une chambre ...** |
| | vōōzôryā äNkôr ēn shäNb'rə ... |

less expensive	**meilleur marché?** meyār märshā?
larger	**plus grande?** plē gräNd?
quieter	**plus tranquille?** plē träNkēl?

| It's very nice. I'll take it. | **Elle me plaît. Je la prends.** |
| | el mə ple. zhə lä präN. |

? **Avez-vous des bagages?**
ävävōō dā bägäzh?   Do you have any luggage?

2

| Can you have my luggage brought to the room? | **Vous pourriez apporter mes bagages dans la chambre?** vōō pōōryā äpôrtā mā bägäzh däN lä shäNb'rə? |

| Can you have a crib put in the room? | **Vous pourriez installer un lit d'enfant?** vōō pōōryā eNstälä eN lē däNfäN? |

| Where can I park my car? | **Où est-ce que je peux garer ma voiture?** ōō eskə zhə pə gärā mä vô·ätēr? |

| Where are the showers? | **Où sont les douches?** ōō sôN lā dōōsh? |

| When are the meals served? | **Quelles sont les heures des repas?** kel sôN lāzār dā rəpä? |

| Where can we get breakfast? | **Où peut-on prendre le petit déjeuner?** ōō pātôN präNd'rə lə pətē dāzhənā? |

39

Can I give you my valuables for safe-keeping?	**Est-ce que je peux vous confier mes objets de valeur?** eska zhə pā vōō kôNfyā māzôbzhe də välär?
I'd like to pick up my valuables.	**Je voudrais reprendre mes objets de valeur.** zhə vōōdre rəpräNd'rə māzôbzhe də välär.
Can you exchange money for me?	**Est-ce que vous pouvez me changer de l'argent?** eska vōō pōōvā mə shäNzhā dəlärzhäN?
May I have the key to room ..., please?	**La clé de la chambre ..., s'il vous plaît.** lä klā dəlä shäNb'rə ..., sēl vōō ple.
Can I make a call to America (from my room)?	**Est-ce que je peux téléphoner aux États-Unis (depuis ma chambre)?** eska zhə pā tālāfônā ōzātāzēnē (dəpē·ē mä shäNb'rə)?
Is there any mail/Are there any messages for me?	**Est-ce qu'il y a du courrier/un message pour moi?** eskēlyä də̄ kōōryā/eN māsäzh pōōr mô·ä?
I'd like a wakeup call (tomorrow) at ... o'clock, please.	**Réveillez-moi (demain) à ... heures, s'il vous plaît.** rāvāyā-mô·ä (dəmeN) ä ... ār, sēl vōō ple.
We're leaving tomorrow.	**Nous partons demain.** nōō pärtôN dəmeN.
Would you please prepare my bill?	**Préparez-nous la note, s'il vous plaît.** prāpärā-nōō lä nôt, sēl vōō ple.

We really liked it here.	**Nous avons passé un séjour très agréable.** nōōzävôN päsä eN säzhōōr trezägrā-äb'lə.
May I leave my luggage here until ... o'clock?	**Est-ce que je peux encore laisser mes bagages ici jusqu'à ... heures?** eskə zhə pā äNkôr läsā mā bägazh ēsē zhẽskä ... ẽr?
Would you call a taxi for me, please?	**Appelez-moi un taxi, s'il vous plaît.** äplā-mô·ä eN täksē, sēl vōō ple.

2

Vacation Rental

We have rented the apartment ...	**Nous avons loué l'appartement ...** nōōzävôN lōō·ā läpärtəmäN ...
Where can we pick up the keys?	**Où pouvons-nous prendre les clés?** ōō pōōvôN-nōō präNd'rə lā klā?
Could you please explain how the ... works?	**Vous pourriez nous expliquer comment fonctionne ..., s'il vous plaît?** vōō pōōryā nōōzeksplēkā kômäN fôNksyôn ... sēl vōō ple?
stove	**la cuisinière** lä kē-ēsēnyer
dishwasher	**le lave-vaisselle** lə läv-vesel
washing machine	**la machine à laver** lä mäshēn ä lävā
Where is the fuse box?	**Où se trouvent les fusibles?** ōō sə trōōv lā fēsēb'lə?

| Where is the meter? | **Où se trouve le compteur électrique?** |
| | ōō sə trōōv lə kôNtạ̄r ālektrēk? |

| Where do we put the trash? | **Où devons-nous déposer les ordures?** |
| | ōō dəvôN-nōō dāpōzā lāzôrdē̲r? |

| Where can I make a phone call? | **Où est-ce qu'on peut téléphoner ici?** |
| | ōō eskôN pạ̄ tālāfónā ēsē? |

| Could you tell us where we might find ... | **Pouvez-vous nous dire où il y a ...** |
| | pōōvā-vōō nōō dēr ōō ēlyä ... |

    a bakery?   **une boulangerie?** ē̲n bōōläNzhərē?

    the nearest bus stop?   **le prochain arrêt de bus?** lə prôshenäre də bēs?

    a grocery store?   **une alimentation?** ē̲n älēmäNtäsyôN?

Complaints

➡ *Please; Thank you (p. 26)*

Please; Thank you (p. 26)

| The *shower/light* doesn't work. | **La *douche/lumière* ne marche pas.** |
| | lä dōōsh/lẹ̄myer nə märsh pä. |

| The toilet doesn't flush. | **La chasse d'eau ne marche pas.** |
| | lä shäs dō nə märsh pä. |

| There is no (hot) water. | **Il n'y a pas d'eau (chaude).** |
| | ēlnyä pä dō (shōd). |

42

Could I please have ...?	**Est-ce que je pourrais avoir encore ..., s'il vous plaît?** eskə zhə pōōre ävô·är äNkôr ..., sēl vōō ple?
another blanket	**une couverture** ēn kōōvertēr
some more dish towels	**des torchons** dā tôrshôN
another towel	**une serviette** ēn servyet
a few more clothes hangers	**quelques cintres** kelkə seNt'rə
I can't lock the door to my room.	**Ma porte ne ferme pas à clé.** mä pôrt nə ferm päzäklā.
The window doesn't *open/close*.	**La fenêtre ne s'ouvre/ferme pas.** lä fənet'rə nə sōōv'rə/ferm pä.
The faucet drips.	**Le robinet goutte.** lə rôbēne gōōt.
The drain is stopped up.	**L'écolement est bouché.** lākōōlmäN e bōōshā.
The toilet is stopped up.	**Les WC sont bouchés.** lā dōōbləvā-sā sôN bōōshā.

2

Hotel and Vacation Rental

adapter	**l'adaptateur** *m* lädäptätēr
additional costs	**les charges** *f/pl* lā shärzh
apartment	**le studio** lə stēdyō
balcony	**le balcon** lə bälkôN
bathroom	**la salle de bains** lä säl də beN
bathtub	**la baignoire** lä benyô·är

43

bed	**le lit** lə lē
– linens	**les draps** *m/pl* lā drä
-sheet	**le drap** lə drä
-side lamp	**la lampe de chevet** lä läNp də shəve
-spread	**le couvre-lit** lə kōōv′rə-lē
bill	**la facture** lä fäktēr
blanket	**la couverture en laine** lä kōōvertēr äN len
breakfast	**le petit déjeuner** lə pətē dāzhānā
– buffet	**le buffet petit déjeuner** lə bēfe pətē dāzhānā
broken	**cassé** käsā
broom	**le balai** lə bäle
cabin	**le bungalow** lə beNgälō
chair	**la chaise** lä shez
cleaning products	**les produits** *m/pl* **de nettoyage** lā prôdē̇-ē də netô-äyäzh
closet	**le placard** lə pläkär
cold water	**l'eau** *f* **froide** lō frô-äd
complaint	**la réclamation** lä räklämäsyôN
crib	**le lit d'enfant** lə lē däNfäN
cup	**la tasse** lä täs
departure	**le départ** lə dāpär
deposit	**la caution** lä kôsyôN
dinner	**le dîner** lə dēnā
dirty	**sale** säl
dishes	**la vaisselle** lä vesel
dishwasher	**le lave-vaisselle** lə läv-vesel
door	**la porte** lä pôrt

door lock	**la serrure** lä serēr
double room	**la chambre pour deux personnes** lä shäNb'rə pōōr dœ̄ persôn
down-payment	**l'acompte** *m* läkôNt
drinking water	**l'eau potable** lō pôtäb'lə
electricity	**l'électricité** *f* lälektrēsētā
elevator	**l'ascenseur** *m* läsäNsœ̄r
extension cable	**la rallonge électrique** lä rälôNzh älektrēk
final cleaning	**le ménage de fin de séjour** lə mänäzh də feN də sāzhōōr
floor	**l'étage** *m* lātäzh
first –	**le rez-de-chaussée** lə rād-shōsā
flush	**la chasse d'eau** lä shäs dō
full price	**le prix T.T.C.** lə prē tā-tā-sā
full room and board,	**la pension complète** lä päNsyôN kôNplet
European plan	
fuse	**le fusible** lə fēzēb'lə
gas cylinder	**la bouteille de butane** lä bōōte'ē̃ də bẽtän
glass	**le verre** lə ver
high season	**la haute saison** lä ōt sezôN
hot water	**l'eau** *f* **chaude** lō shōd
hotel	**l'hôtel** *m* lōtel
key	**la clé** lä klā
lamp	**la lampe** lä läNp
light bulb	**l'ampoule** *f* läNpōōl
lost	**perdu** perdē
low season	**la basse saison** lä bäs sezôN

luggage	**les bagages** *m/pl* lā bägäzh
lunch	**le déjeuner** lə dāzhǎnā
maid	**la femme de chambre** lä fäm də shäNb'rə
mattress	**le matelas** lə mátlä
outlet	**la prise (de courant)** lä prēz (də kōōräN)
pillow	**l'oreiller** *m* lôrāyā
plate	**l'assiette** *f* läsyet
plug	**la fiche** lä fēsh
pool	**la piscine** lä pēsēn
pre-season	**l'avant-saison** *f* läväN-sezôN
reception	**la réception** lä rāsepsyôN
refrigerator	**le réfrigérateur** lə räfrēzhärätǎr
rent	**le loyer** lə lô-äyā
to rent	**louer** lōō·ā
(rented vacation) apartment	**le meublé** lə mäblā
(rented vacation) house	**la maison de vacances** lä mezôN də väkäNs
to reserve	**réserver** rāzervā
reserved	**réservé** rāzervā
room	**la chambre** lä shäNb'rə
– inventory	**l'état** *m* **des lieux** lätä dā lēyǎ
– with half board	**la demi-pension** lä dəmē-päNsyôN
shower	**la douche** lä dōōsh
single room	**la chambre pour une personne** lä shäNb'rə pōōr ēn persôn
sink *(bathroom)*	**le lavabo** lə läväbō

46

sink *(kitchen)*	**l'évier** *m* lāvyā
stairs	**les escaliers** *m/pl* lāzeskälyā
stopped up	**bouché** bōōshā
table	**la table** lä täb'əl
tax on visitors	**la taxe de séjour** lä täks də sāzhōōr
telephone	**le téléphone** lə tālāfôn
toilet	**les toilettes** *f/pl* lā tô·älet
– paper	**le papier hygiénique** lə päpyā ēzhē·änēk
towel	**la serviette** lä servyet
trash	**les ordures** *f/pl* lāzôrdēr
– can	**la poubelle** lä pōōbel
to wake	**réveiller** rāvāyā
water	**l'eau** *f* lō
– faucet	**le robinet** lə rôbēne
window	**la fenêtre** lä fənet'rə
to work	**fonctionner** fôNksyônā

2

YOUTH HOSTEL, CAMPING

Youth Hostel

Is there anything available?	**Est-ce que vous avez encore quelque chose de libre?** eskə vōōzävä äNkôr kelkə shōz də lēb'rə?
I would like to stay for *one night / ... nights.*	**Je voudrais rester** *une nuit/... nuits.* zhə vōōdre restā ēn nē·ē/... nē·ē.
How much will it cost for one night?	**Combien coûte une nuit?** kôNbyeN kōōt ēn nē·ē?

47

Do you also have double rooms?	**Vous avez aussi des chambres pour deux personnes?** vōōzävā ōsē dā shäNb'rə pōōr dā̄ persôn?
Is breakfast included?	**Le petit déjeuner est compris?** lə pətē dāzh̲ā̲nā ā kôNprē?
How much does ... cost?	**Combien coûte le ...** kôNbyeN kōōt lə ...
breakfast	**petit déjeuner?** pətē dāzh̲ā̲nā?
lunch	**déjeuner?** dāzh̲ā̲nā?
dinner	**dîner?** dēnā?
Where is the dining room?	**Où est la salle à manger?** ōō e lä säl ä mäNzh̲ā?
Where can I buy something *to eat*/*to drink*?	**Où est-ce qu'on peut acheter quelque chose à *manger*/*boire* ici?** ōō eskôN pā äshtā kelkə shōz ä *mäNzh̲ā*/*bó·àr* ēsē?
Where are the meals served?	**Quelles sont les heures des repas?** kel sôN lāzā̲r dā rəpä?
Where are the bath-rooms?	**Où sont les lavabos?** ōō sôN lā läväbō?
Where is the rest-room?	**Où sont les toilettes?** ōō sôN lā tô·àlet?
Where can I do my laundry?	**Où est-ce qu'on peut laver son linge?** ōō eskôN pā lävā sôN leNzh̲?

When do I have to be back by?	**Jusqu'à quelle heure est-ce qu'on peut rentrer le soir?** zhēskä kelär eskôN pā räNtrā lə sô·är?
Do you have any lockers?	**Il y a des casiers fermant à clé?** ēlyä dā käzyā fermäNtä klā?
What's the best way to get to the middle of town?	**Quel est le meilleur moyen pour aller dans le centre?** kel e lə meyär mô·äyeN pōōr älä däN lə säNt'rə?

Camping

May we camp on your property?	**Est-ce que nous pouvons camper sur votre terrain?** eskə nōō pōōvôN käNpä sēr vôt'rə tereN?
What is the charge for ...	**Quel est le tarif pour ...** kel e lə tärēf pōōr ...
a car with a trailer?	**une voiture avec caravane?** ēn vô·ätēr ävek kärävän?
a camping van? a tent?	**un camping-car?** eN käNpēng-kär? **une tente?** ēn täNt?
We'd like a (sheltered) place in the shade.	**Nous voudrions un emplacement à l'ombre (abrité du vent).** nōō vōōdrē·ôN eNäNpläsmäN älôNb'rə (äbrētā dē väN).
We'd like to stay *one night/... nights.*	**Nous voudrions rester *un jour/... jours.*** nōō vōōdrē·ôN restä *eN zhōōr/... zhōōr.*

2

49

Where are the bathrooms?	**Où sont les lavabos?** ōō sôN lā lāvābō?
Where is the rest room?	**Où sont les toilettes?** ōō sôN lā tô-ä-let?
Where can I ...	**Où est-ce qu'on peut ...** ōō eskôN pā ...
empty the chemical waste from the toilet?	**vidanger les WC chimiques?** vēdäNzhā lā dōōblevä-sā shēmēk?
empty sewage water?	**se débarrasser des eaux usées?** sə dābäräsā dāzō ēzā?
fill the tank with fresh water?	**refaire le plein d'eau?** rəfer lə pleN dō?
Can I use electricity?	**Vous avez un branchement électrique?** vōōzävā eN bräNshmäN ālektrēk?
Is there a grocery store here?	**Est-ce qu'il y a une alimentation par ici?** eskēlyä ēn älēmäNtäsyôN pär ēsē?
Can I *rent/exchange* gas cylinder here?	**Je peux *emprunter/échanger* des bouteilles de butane ici?** zhə pā *äNpreNtā/āshäNzhā* dā bōōte'ē də bētän ēsē?
May I borrow a(n) ..., please?	**Vous pourriez me prêter ..., s'il vous plaît?** vōō pōōryā mə prātā ..., sēl vōō ple?

air mattress	**le matelas pneumatique** lə mätlä pnāmätēk
bed linens	**les draps** *m/pl* lā drä
to borrow	**emprunter** äNpreNtā
camping	**le camping** lə käNpēng
– permit	**la carte de camping** lä kärt də käNpēng
campsite	**le terrain de camping** lə tereN də käNpēng
check-in	**la déclaration de séjour** lä dāklärāsyôN də sāzhōōr
to cook	**faire la cuisine** fer lä kē̄-ēzēn
cooking utensils	**les ustensiles** *m/pl* **de cuisine** läzē̄stäNsēl də kē̄-ēzēn
detergent	**la lessive** lä lesēv
dormitory	**le dortoir** lə dôrtô·är
electrical outlet	**la prise (de courant)** lä prēz (də kōōräN)
electricity	**le courant (électrique)** lə kōōräN (ālektrēk)
foam (insulation) mat	**le matelas mini-mousse** lə mätlä mēnē-mōōs
gas	**le gaz** lə gäz
– canister	**la cartouche de gaz** lä kärtōōsh də gäz
– cylinder	**la bouteille de butane** lä bōōtā'ē də bētän
group of kids	**le groupe de jeunes** lə grōōp də zhän
hostel father	**le père aubergiste** lə per ōberzhēst

2

hostel mother	**la mère aubergiste** lä mer ōberzhēst
to iron	**repasser** rəpäsā
mallet	**le maillet** lə mäye
playground	**le terrain de jeux** lə tereN də zhā
rental fee	**les frais** *m/pl* **d'utilisation**
	lā fre dētēlēzäsyôN
reservation	**la réservation** lä rāzerväsyôN
room	**la chambre** lä shäNb'rə
shower	**la douche** lä dōōsh
site	**l'emplacement** *m* läNpläsmäN
sleeping bag	**le sac de couchage** lə säk də kōōshäzh
stove	**le réchaud** lə rāshō
tent	**la tente** lä täNt
– peg	**le piquet (de tente)** lə pēke (də täNt)
– pole	**le mât de tente** lə mä də täNt
toilet	**les toilettes** *f/pl* lā tô-älet
to wash	**laver** lävā
washing machine	**la machine à laver** lä mäshēn ä lävā
washroom	**les lavabos** *m/pl* lā läväbō
water	**l'eau** *f* lō
– canister	**le jerricane à eau** lə dzherēkän ä ō
youth hostel	**l'auberge** *f* **de jeunesse**
	lōberzh də zhānes
– card	**la carte d'auberge de jeunesse**
	lä kärt dōberzh də zhānes

On the Way

ASKING THE WAY

Excuse me, where is ...?	**Pardon, où est ...?** pärdôN, ōō e ...?
How can I get to ...?	**Pour aller à ...?** pōōr älä ä ...?
What's the *quickest/ cheapest* way to get to the ...	**Quel est le moyen *le plus rapide/le moins cher* pour aller ...** kele lə mô·äyeN *lə plē räpēd/lə mô·eN sher* pōōr älä ...
train station?	**à la gare?** ä lä gär?
bus station?	**à la gare routière?** ä lä gär rōōtyer?
airport?	**à l'aéroport?** ä lä·ärōpôr?

! **Le mieux, c'est de prendre un taxi.** lə myā, se də präNd(rə) eN täksē.   The best thing to do is take a taxi.

! **Là-bas.** lä-bä.   Over there.

! **En arrière.** äNäryer.   Go back.

! **Tout droit.** tōō drô·ä.   Straight ahead.

! **A droite.** ä drô·ät.   To the right.

! **A gauche.** ä gōsh.   To the left.

54

	La *première/deuxième* rue à *gauche/droite.* lä prəmyer/ dāzyem rē ä gōsh/drô·āt.	The *first/second* street to the *left/right.*
! •	**Au feu.** ō fē.	At the traffic lights.
! •	**Après le carrefour.** äpre lə kärfōōr.	After the intersection.
	Traversez ... träversā ...	Cross ...
! •	**le pont.** lə pôN. **la place.** lä pläs. **la rue.** lä rē.	the bridge. the square. the street.
! •	**Après, vous redemanderez.** äpre, vōō rədəmäNdrā.	When you get there, ask again.
	Vous pouvez prendre ... vōō pōōvā präNd'rə ...	You can take ...
! •	**le bus.** lə bēs. **le tramway.** lə trämōō·ā. **le RER.** lə er-ə-er.	the bus. the streetcar. the commuter train.
	le métro. lə mātrō.	the subway.

3

Is this the road to ...?	**C'est bien la route de ...?** se byeN lä rōōt də ...?	
How far is it?	**C'est à quelle distance?** setäkel dēstäNs?	
! •	**Assez loin.** äsā lô·eN.	Pretty far.

55

! **Pas loin.** pä lô·eN.   Not (very) far.

How many minutes   **Combien de minutes à pied?**
will it take to walk?   kôNbyeN də mināt ä pyā?

Could you show it to   **Vous pouvez me le montrer sur la**
me on the map?   **carte, s'il vous plaît?** vōō pōōvā mə lə
                        môNtrā sȳr lä kärt, sēl vōō ple?

Asking the Way

bridge	**le pont** lə pôN
to cross	**traverser** trävsā
curve	**le virage** lə vēräzh
intersection	**le carrefour** lə kärfōōr
road	**la route** lä rōōt
straight ahead	**tout droit** tōō drô·ä
street	**la rue** lä rā
to the left	**à gauche** ä gōsh
to the right	**à droite** ä drô·ät
traffic lights	**le feu** lə fā

AT THE BORDER

Passport Control

! **Vos papiers, s'il vous**   May I see your docu-
• **plaît.** vō päpyā, sēl vōō ple.   ments, please?

! **Votre passeport, s'il vous plaît.**   May I see your pass-
• vôt'rə päspôr, sēl vōō ple.   port, please?

! **•**	**Votre passeport est périmé.** vôt'rə pàspôr e pārēmā.	Your passport is expired.

I'm with the ... group.	**Je fais partie du groupe ...** zhə fe pàrtē dē grōōp ...	

Customs

? **•**	**Avez-vous quelque chose à déclarer?** àvā-vōō kelkə shōz à dāklàrā?	Do you have anything to declare?

! **•**	**Ouvrez votre *coffre/valise*, s'il vous plaît.** ōōvrā vôt'rə *kôf'rə/ vàlēz*, sēl vōō ple.	Open your *trunk/suitcase*, please.

! **•**	**Vous devez le déclarer.** vōō dəvā lə dāklàrā.	You have to declare that.

3

At the Border

bill	**la facture** là fàktēr
border	**la frontière** là frôNtyer
car registration	**les papiers *m/pl* de voiture** lā pàpyā də vô·àtēr
country identification sticker	**la plaque de nationalité** là plàk də nàsyônàlētā
customs	**la douane** là dōō·àn
– declaration	**la déclaration de douane** là dāklàràsyôN də dōō·àn
– office	**le bureau de douane** lə bērō də dōō·àn
date	**la date** là dàt

57

to declare	**déclarer** däklärā
driver's license	**le permis de conduire**
	lə permē də kôNdē̲-ēr
first name	**le prénom** lə prānôN
ID	**la carte d'identité** lä kärt dēdäNtētā
inoculation record	**le carnet de vaccination**
	lə kärne də väksēnäsyôN
invalid	**pas valable** pä väläb'lə
last name	**le nom de famille** lə nôN də fämē̲'ē̲
nationality	**la nationalité** lä näsyônälētā
number	**le numéro** lə nēmārō
papers	**les papiers** *m/pl* lā päpyā
passport	**le passeport** lə päspôr
– control	**le contrôle des passeports**
	lə kôNtrôl dā päspôrt
place of residence	**le domicile** lə dômēsēl
to renew	**prolonger** prôlôNzhā
signature	**la signature** lä sēnyätēr
tour group	**le groupe (de touristes)**
	lə grōōp (də tōōrēst)
valid	**valable** väläb'lə
value-added tax	**la TVA** lä tā-vā-ä
(VAT)	

LUGGAGE

May I *leave/pick up* my luggage here?
Je voudrais *laisser mes bagages ici/retirer mes bagages.* zhə vōōdre lāsā mā bägäzh ēsē/rəfērā mā bägäzh.

May I leave my back-pack with you *for an hour/until* ...?
Est-ce que je peux laisser mon sac à dos ici *pour une heure/jusqu'à ...*? eskə zhə pā lāsā môN säk ä dō ēsē pōōr ēnär/zhēskä ...?

I'd like to have these bags sent to ...
Je voudrais faire enregistrer ces baga-ges pour ... zhə vōōdre fer äNrzhēstrā sā bägäzh pōōr ...

When will they be at ... ?
Quand seront-ils à ...? käN sərôNtēl ä ...?

My luggage hasn't arrived (yet).
Mes bagages ne sont pas (encore) arrivés. mā bägäzh nə sôN pä (äNkôr) ärēvā.

Where is my luggage?
Où sont mes bagages? ōō sôN mā bägäzh?

A suitcase is missing.
Il manque une valise. ēl mäNk ēn välēz.

My luggage has been damaged.
Ma valise a été abîmée. mä välēz ä ātā äbēmā.

Who can I report it to?
A qui est-ce que je peux m'adresser? äkē eskə zhə pā mädräsā?

59

backpack	**le sac à dos** lə säk ä dō
bag	**le sac** lə säk
baggage claim	**le retrait des bagages** lə rətre dā bägäzh
baggage ticket	**le bulletin d'enregistrement** lə bēlteN däNrzhēstrəmäN
carry-on luggage	**les bagages** *m/pl* **à main** lā bägäzh ä meN
excess luggage	**l'excédent** *m* **de bagages** leksädäN də bägäzh
flight bag	**le sac de voyage** lə säk də vô·äyäzh
to hand in	**faire enregistrer** fer äNrzhēstrā
locker	**la consigne automatique** lä kôNsēnyôtômätēk
luggage	**les bagages** *m/pl* lä bägäzh
– check-in	**l'enregistrement** *m* **des bagages** läNrzhēstrəmäN dā bägäzh
– storage	**la consigne** lä kôNsēn'yə
to pick up	**retirer** rətērā
suitcase	**la valise** lä välēz

PLANE

Information and Booking

Where is the ... counter?	**Où est le guichet de ...?** ōō e lə gēshe də ...?
When is the next flight to ...?	**A quelle heure est le prochain vol pour ...?** äkelär e lə prôsheN vôl pōōr ...?

60

When will a plane be flying to ... today/ tomorrow?	**A quelle heure y a-t-il** *aujourd'hui/ demain* **un vol pour ...?** äkelār ēyätēl ōzhōōrdvē/dəmeN eN vôl pōōr ...?
When will we be in ...?	**A quelle heure arrive-t-on à ...?** äkelār ärēvtôN ä ...?
How much will it cost to fly to ... (round trip)?	**Combien coûte un vol (aller-retour) pour ...?** kôNbyeN kōōt eN vôl (älā-rətōōr) pōōr ...?
I'd like a ticket to ..., ...	**Un billet pour ..., s'il vous plaît.** eN bēye pōōr ..., sēl vōō ple.

? **Aller simple ou aller-retour?**
älā seNp'lə ōō älā-rətōōr?

One way or round trip?

? **Classe économie, classe affaires ou première classe?** kläs ākônōmē, kläs äfer ōō prəmyer kläs?

Economy, business or first class?

! **Ce vol est malheureusement complet.** sə vôl e mälərāzmäN kôNple.

I'm afraid this flight is sold out.

Are there any *special rates/stand-by seats* available?	**Est-ce qu'il y a des** *tarifs spéciaux/ places stand by***?** eskēlyä dā tärēf spāsyō/pläs stäNd-bä'ē?

3

| I'd like ... | **Je voudrais une place ...** |
| | zhə vōōdre ẽn pläs ... |

a window seat.	**fenêtre.** fənet'rə.
an aisle seat.	**couloir.** kōōlô·är.
a seat in nonsmok-	**non-fumeurs.** nôN-fē̅mār.
ing.	
a seat in smoking.	**fumeurs.** fē̅mār.

| Where is Gate B? | **Où est la sortie B?** ōō e lä sôrtē bā? |

| I'd like to ... my | **Je voudrais ... mon vol.** |
| flight. | zhə vōōdre ... môN vôl. |

confirm	**faire confirmer** fer kôNfērmā
cancel	**annuler** änē̅lā
change	**modifier** môdēfyā

On the Plane

Could I have *(another/*	**Est-ce que je peux avoir (encore) ...,**
some more) ..., please?	**s'il vous plaît?** eskə zhə pā̈ ävô·är
	(äNkôr) ..., sēl vōō ple?

| I feel sick. | **J'ai mal au cœur.** zhā mäl ō kār. |

Do you have	**Est-ce que vous avez un remède**
something for air	**contre le mal de l'air?** eskə vōōzävā
sickness?	eN rəmed kôNtrə lə mäl də ler?

air sickness bag	**le sachet vomitoire** lə säshe vômētô·är
airline	**la compagnie aérienne** lä kôNpänyē ä·ärē·en
airplane	**l'avion** *m* lävyôN
airport	**l'aéroport** *m* lä·ārōpôr
arrival	**l'arrivée** *f* lärēvā
to book	**réserver** rāzervā
to cancel	**annuler** änēlā
to change	**modifier** môdēfyā
charter flight	**le vol charter** lə vôl shärter
class	**la classe** lä kläs
to confirm	**confirmer** kôNfērmā
counter	**le guichet** lə gēshe
delay	**le retard** lə rətär
departure	**le départ** lə dāpär
desk	**le guichet** lə gēshe
exit	**la sortie** lä sôrtē
flight	**le vol** le vôl
– attendant *(male)*	**le steward** lə styōō·ärd
– attendant *(female)*	**l'hôtesse** *f* **de l'air** lōtes də ler
to fly	**voler** vôlā
carry-on luggage	**les bagages** *m/pl* **à main** lā bägäzh ä meN
information desk	**le guichet d'information** lə gēshe deNfôrmäsyôN
local time	**l'heure** *f* **locale** lār lôkäl

3

63

nonsmoking	**le non-fumeur** lə nôN-fēmār
return flight	**le vol de retour** lə vôl də rətōōr
scheduled flight	**le vol de ligne** lə vôl də lēn'yə
smoking	**le fumeur** lə fēmār
stopover	**l'escale** *f* leskäl
ticket	**le billet** lə bēye

RAIL

Information and Tickets

At which station can I get a train to ...?	**Pour aller à ..., je dois partir de quelle gare?** pōōr älā ä ..., zhə dô·ä .pärtēr də kel gär?
Where is the *train/ tourist* information office?	**Où sont les renseignements/est l'office du tourisme?** ōō sôN lā räNsen'yəmäN/ e lôfēs dē tōōrēsm?
Where can I find the *luggage storage/ lockers?*	**Où est la *consigne/consigne automatique?*** ōō e lä kôNsēn'yə/ kôNsēnyótômätēk?
When is the *next/last* train to ...?	**A quelle heure part le *prochain/dernier* train pour ...?** äkelār pär lə prôsheN/dernyā treN pōōr ...?
When will it arrive in ...?	**A quelle heure arrive-t-il à ...?** äkelār ärēvtēl ä ...?
When are the trains to ...?	**Quand y a-t-il des trains pour ...?** käN yätēl dā treN pōōr ...?

Do I have to change trains?	**Est-ce que je dois changer?** eskə zhə dô·ä shäNzhā?
Which platform does the train to ... leave from?	**De quel quai part le train pour ...?** də kel kā pär lə treN pōōr ...?
How much does a ticket to ... cost?	**Combien coûte un billet pour ...?** kôNbyeN kōōt eN bēye pōōr ...?
Are there special rates for ...?	**Est-ce qu'il y a des réductions pour ...?** eskēlyä dā rādēksyôN pōōr ...?
Do you have to pay extra for this train?	**Est-ce que ce train est à supplément?** eskə sə treN etä sēplämäN?
I'd like *a ticket/two tickets* to ..., ... please.	**Un billet/Deux billets pour ..., s'il vous plaît, ...** eN bēye/dē̲ bēye pōōr ..., sēl vōō ple ...
first/second class	*première/deuxième* **classe.** prəmyer/dē̲zyem kläs.
for children	**pour enfants.** pōōr äNfäN.
for adults	**pour adultes.** pōōr ädēlt.

? **Aller simple ou aller-retour?** älā seNp'lə ōō älā-rətōōr?   One way or round trip?

| I'd like to reserve a seat on the ... o'clock train to ..., please. | **Réservez-moi une place dans le train de ... heures pour ..., s'il vous plaît.** rāzervā-mô·ä ēn pläs däN lə treN də ... ār pōōr ..., sēl vōō ple. |

3

? **Compartiment ou voiture salle?** Compartment or open
kôNpärtēmäN ōō vô·ätēr säl? seating?

I'd like a seat ... **J'aimerais avoir une place ...**
zhāməre ävô·är ēn pläs ...

by the window. **fenêtre.** fənet'rə.
in nonsmoking. **non-fumeurs.** nôN-fēmär.
in smoking. **fumeurs.** fēmär.

INFO In France you must stamp your ticket at one of the
machines (**composteurs**) standing at the entrance
to the platforms before you begin your journey.

Information

Accès aux quais äkse ō kä	To All Trains
Consigne kôNsēn'yə	Baggage Storage
Consigne automatique	Lockers
kôNsēnyôtômätēk	
Enregistrement des bagages	Baggage Check-In
äNrzhēstrəmäN dā bägäzh	
Lavabos läväbō	Washrooms
Renseignements räNsenyəmäN	Information
Restaurant de la gare	Restaurant
restôräN də lä gär	
Salle d'attente säl dätäNt	Waiting Room
Sortie sôrtē	Exit
Toilettes tô·älet	Rest Rooms
Voie vô·ä	Track

66

On the Train

May I sit here?	**Est-ce que cette place est libre?** eskə set pläs e lēb'rə
Excuse me, but I believe this is my seat.	**Excusez-moi, c'est ma place.** ekskēzā-mô·ä, se mä pläs.
Would you mind if I opened/closed the window?	**Vous permettez que j'ouvre/je ferme la fenêtre?** vōō permetā ke zhōōv'rə)/ferm lä fənet'rə?

! **Les billets, s'il vous plaît!**   Tickets, please!
  lā bēye, sēl vōō ple!

How many more stops to ...?	**Combien y a-t-il encore d'arrêts jusqu'à ...?** kôNbyeN yätēl äNkôr däre zhēskä ...?
How long is our layover?	**Combien de temps dure l'arrêt?** kôNbyeN də täN dēr läre?
Will I be in time to catch the train to ...?	**Est-ce que j'aurai le train de ...?** eskə zhôrā lə treN də ...?

3

Train

arrival	**l'arrivée** f lärēvā
car	**la voiture, le wagon** lä vô·ätēr, lə vägôN
to change (trains)	**changer de train** shäNzhā də treN
class	**la classe** lä kläs
compartment	**le compartiment** lə kôNpärtēmäN
connection	**la correspondance** lä kôrespôNdäNs
departure	**le départ** lə dāpär

67

dining car	**le wagon-restaurant** lə vägôN-restôräN
discount	**la réduction** lä rādēksyôN
exit	**la sortie** lä sôrtē
extra cost	**le supplément** lə sēplämäN
family compartment	**le compartiment «Espace-enfants»** lə kôNpärtēmäN espäs-äNfäN
fare	**le prix du billet** lə prē dᵫ bēye
to get off	**descendre** dāsäNd'rə
to get on	**monter** môNtā
platform	**le quai** lə kā
reserved	**réservé** rāzervā
seat	**la place** lä pläs
sleeper *(many beds)*	**la voiture-couchettes** lä vô·ätēr-kōōshet
sleeper *(1– 4 beds)*	**le wagon-lit** lə vägôN-lē
stop	**l'arrêt** *m* läre
taken	**occupé** ôkēpā
through car	**la voiture directe** lä vô·ätēr dērekt
ticket	**le billet** lə bēye
timetable	**l'horaire** *m* lôrer
track	**la voie** lä vô·ä
train	**le train** lə treN
– station	**la gare** lä gär

BOAT

Information and Booking

When will there be a
ship/ferry going to ...?
...?

**Quand y a-t-il un *bateau/ferry*
pour ...?** käN yätēl eN *bätō/ferē* pōōr
...?

How long is the
passage to ...?

**Combien de temps dure la traversée
pour ...?** kôNbyeN də täN dēr lä
träversā pōōr ...?

When must we be on
board?

Quand devons-nous être à bord?
käN dəvôN-nōō eträ bôr?

I'd like to board with
a car.

Je voudrais embarquer une voiture.
zhə vōōdre äNbärkā ēn vô·ätēr.

I'd like a *first class/
tourist class* ticket
to ...

**Je voudrais un billet de bateau *pre-
mière classe/classe touriste* pour ...**
zhə vōōdre eN bēye də bätō *prəmyer
kläs/kläs tōōrēst* pōōr ...

3

I'd like a ticket for
the excursion at ...
o'clock.

**Je voudrais un billet pour l'excursion
de ... heures.** zhə vōōdre eN bēye pōōr
lekskērsyóN də ... ār.

Where has the ...
docked?

Où est accosté le ...? ōō etäkôstā lə ...?

69

On Board

I'm looking for cabin number ...	**Je cherche la cabine numéro ...** zhə shersh lä käbēn nē̮mārō ...
May I have a different cabin?	**Est-ce que je pourrais changer de cabine?** eskə zhə pōōre shäNzhā də käbēn?
Do you have something for sea-sickness?	**Vous avez un remède contre le mal de mer?** vōōzävä eN rəmed kôNt'rə lə mäl də mer?

Boat

air conditioning	**l'air *m* conditionné** ler kôNdēsyônā
blanket	**la couverture** lä kōōvertēr̮
boat-trip	**la croisière** lä krô·äzyer
cabin	**la cabine** lä käbēn
canal	**le canal** lə känäl
captain	**le capitaine** lə käpēten
car ferry	**le car-ferry** lə kär-ferē
coast	**la côte** lä kōt
deck	**le pont** lə pôN
dining hall	**la salle à manger** lə säl ä mäNzhā
double cabin	**la cabine double** lä käbēn dōōb'lə
drawbridge	**le pont levant** lə pôN ləväN
exterior cabin	**la cabine extérieure** lä käbēn ekstāryär̮
ferry	**le ferry** lə ferē
four-bed cabin	**la cabine à quatre personnes** lä käbēn ä kät'rə persôn

hovercraft	**l'hydroglisseur** *m* lēdrōglēsǎr
interior cabin	**la cabine intérieure** lä käbēn eNtāryǎr
island	**l'île** *f* lēl
land excursion	**l'excursion** *f* **à terre**
	leksk<u>e</u>rsyôN ä ter
landing	**le point d'accostage**
	lə pô·eN däkôstäzh
lifeboat	**l'embarcation** *f* **de sauvetage**
	läNbärkäsyôN də sōvtäzh
life vest	**le gilet de sauvetage**
	lə zhēle də sōvtäzh
lock	**l'écluse** *f* lākl<u>e</u>z
lounge chair	**la chaise longue** lä shez lôNg
passage	**la traversée** lä träversā
port	**le port** lə pôr
rough sea	**la mer agitée** lä mer äzhētā
sea	**la mer** lä mer
sea-sickness	**le mal de mer** lə mäl də mer
ship	**le bateau** lə bätō
ship's agent	**l'agence** *f* **maritime** läzhäNs märētēm
shore	**le rivage** lə rēväzh
single cabin	**la cabine individuelle**
	lä käbēn eNdēvēdē̱·el
steward	**le steward** lə styōō·ärd
sun deck	**le sundeck** lə sǎndek
swimming pool	**la piscine** lä pēsēn
trip	**l'excursion** *f* leksk<u>e</u>rsyôN

3

71

CAR, MOTORBIKE AND BIKE

Rentals

I'd like to rent a ... (with automatic transmission).

Je voudrais louer ... (avec changement de vitesses automatique). zhe vōōdre lōō·ā ... (ävek shäNzhmäN de vëtes ôtômätēk).

car	**une voiture** ēn vô·ätēr
four-wheel drive	**un 4×4** eN kät're kät're
van	**un minibus** eN mēnēbēs
motorcycle	**une moto** ēn mōtō
motor home	**un camping-car** eN käNpēng-kär

INFO The RN (**route nationale**) is comparable to an interstate road, the RD (**route départementale**) to a state road.

You may drive up to 50 km/hour (30 mph) within towns, up to 90 km/hour (55 mph) on state roads without a center stripe, and up to 110 km/hour (65 mph) on state roads with a passing lane or center stripe. You may accelerate up to 110 km/hour on the city highways and up to 130 km/hour (75 mph) on the other French national highways.

? **Est-ce que je pourrais voir votre permis de conduire (international)?** eske zhe pōōre vô·är vôt're permē de kôNdē̄·ēr (eNternäsyônäl)?

May I see your (international) driver's license, please?

I'd like to rent a bicycle/mountain bike (with back-pedal brakes).	**Je voudrais louer** *une bicyclette/un V.T.T.* **(avec rétropédalage).** zhə vōōdre lōō·ā ēn bēsēklet/eN vā-tā-tā (ávek rātrôpādäläz).	
I'd like to rent it (for) ...	**Je voudrais louer la voiture pour ...** zhə vōōdre lōō·ā lä vô·ätēr pōōr ...	
tomorrow.	**demain.** dəmeN.	
the day after tomorrow.	**après-demain.** äpre-dəmeN.	
one day.	**une journée.** ēn zhōōrnā.	
one week.	**une semaine.** ēn səmen.	

? **Quelle sorte de voiture désirez-vous?** kel sôrt də vô·ätēr dāzērā-vōō? — What kind of car would you like?

3

How much does it cost? — **Combien ça coûte?** kôNbyeN sä kōōt?

How much mileage is included in the price? — **Combien de kilomètres sont inclus dans le prix?** kôNbyeN də kēlômet'rə sôNteNklē däN lə prē?

INFO French national highways are toll roads. You must pay the toll at the (automatic) toll booths (**péage (automatique)**). Before you drive up you will see signs that say **"Péage. Préparez votre monnaie."** – "Toll approaching. Please have exact change ready." If you don't have the exact amount, drive into the lane marked **"Usagers sans monnaie"** – "Drivers without exact change."

What kind of fuel does it take?	**Quelle sorte de carburant est-ce-qu'elle consomme?** kel sôrt də kärbȩräN eskel kôNsôm?
Is comprehensive insurance included?	**L'assurance tous risques est comprise?** läsȩräNs tōō rēsk e kôNprēz?
How much is the deductible?	**A combien s'élève la franchise?** ä kôNbyeN sälev lä fräNshēz?
Can I return the car in ...?	**Je peux aussi restituer la voiture à ...?** zhə pȩ ôsē restētȩ·ä lä vô·ätȩr ä ...?
When do I have to be back?	**A quelle heure est-ce que je dois être de retour?** äkelȩr eskə zhə dô·ä et'rə də rətōōr?
I'd also like a helmet.	**Donnez-moi aussi un casque de protection, s'il vous plaît.** dônā-mô·ä ôsē eN käsk də prôteksyôN, sēl vōō ple.

Parking

| Is there a parking *garage/lot* nearby? | **Est-ce qu'il y a un *parking couvert/ parking par ici?** eskēlyä eN *pärkēng kōōvär/pärkēng* pär ēsē? |
| Is the parking lot supervised? | **Est-ce que le parking est gardé?** eskə lə pärkēng e gärdā? |

INFO In France there is often a limit to the length of time you may leave your car parked somewhere. Frequently you must get a parking receipt from one of the parking timer machines: **"Prenez un ticket à l'horodateur."**

Is the parking garage open all night?	**Est-ce que le parking est ouvert toute la nuit?** eskə lə pärkēng etōōver tōōt lä nē̄-ē?
Can I park here?	**Je peux me garer ici?** zhə pā̃ mə gàrā ēsē?

Gas Stations, Car Repair

Where is/How far is it to the nearest gas station?	**Où/À quelle distance se trouve la station-service la plus proche?** ōō/ä kel dēstäNs sə trōōv lä stäsyôN-servēs lä plē prôsh?
... euros' worth of ..., please.	**Pour ... euros ..., s'il vous plaît.** pōōr ... ā̄rō' ..., sēl vōō ple.
unleaded	**d'ordinaire sans plomb** dôrdēnär säN plôN
diesel	**de gazole** də gàzôl
leaded	**d'ordinaire** dôrdēnär
super unleaded	**de super sans plomb** də sēpär säN plôN
super leaded	**de super avec plomb** də sēpär ävek plôN
two-stroke engine fuel	**de mélange deux-temps** də mäläNzh dā-täN.

3

75

| Fill it up, please. | **Le plein, s'il vous plaît.** |
| | lə pleN, sēl vōō ple. |

| I'd like *1 liter*/*2 liters* of oil, please. | **Je voudrais *1 litre*/*2 litres* d'huile.** |
| | zhə vōōdre eN lēt'rə/dā lēt'rə dē-ēl. |

| Could you change the oil, please? | **Une vidange, s'il vous plaît.** |
| | ēN vēdäNzh, sēl vōō ple. |

| I need snow chains. | **Il me faudrait des chaînes (à neige).** |
| | ēl mə fōdre dā shen (ä nezh). |

Breakdown and Accidents

| Please call ..., quickly! | **Vite, appelez ...** vēt, äplā ... |

the fire department	**les pompiers!** lā pôNpyā!
an ambulance	**une ambulance!** ēn äNbēläNs!
the police	**la police!** lā pôlēs!

| I've had an accident. | **J'ai eu un accident.** |
| | zhā ē enäksēdäN. |

| May I use your phone? | **Je peux téléphoner de chez vous?** |
| | zhə pē tālāfônā də shā vōō? |

| Nobody's hurt. | **Personne n'est blessé.** |
| | persôn ne blesā. |

| ... people have been (seriously) injured. | **Il y a ... blessés (graves).** |
| | ēlyä ... blesā (gräv). |

76

Please help me.	**Aidez-moi, s'il vous plaît.**
	ādā-mô·á, sēl vōō ple.
I need some bandages.	**J'ai besoin de pansements.**
	zhā bezô·eN də päNsmäN.
I'm out of gas.	**Je suis en panne sèche.**
	zhə svē äN pän sesh.
The radiator's over-heating.	**L'eau du radiateur bout.**
	lō dȩ̄ rädyätȩ̄r bōō.
Could you ...	**Est-ce que vous pourriez ...**
	eskə vōō pōōryā ...
give me a lift?	**m'emmener un bout de chemin?**
	mämnā eN bōō də shəmeN?
tow my car?	**remorquer ma voiture?**
	rəmôrkā mä vô·ätȩ̄r?
send me a tow-truck?	**m'envoyer la dépanneuse?**
	mäNvô·äyā lä dāpänȩ̄z?
It's not my fault.	**Ce n'est pas de ma faute.**
	sə ne pä də mä fōt.
I think we should get the police.	**Je voudrais que l'on appelle la police.**
	zhə vōōdre ke lônäpel lä pôlēs.
I was doing ... kilo-meters an hour.	**Je faisais du ...** zhə fəze dȩ̄ ...

3

INFO One does not usually get in touch with the police after a minor "fender bender" accident in France. It is sufficient for both parties to fill out and sign an accident form (**constat à l'amiable**), complete with a sketch. If possible, include the names and addresses of any witnesses. Send this form to your insurance company; this does not signify acceptance of responsibility for the accident. If the parties involved cannot come to an agreement, however, then it would be advisable to call the police.

You didn't have the right-of-way.	**Vous n'avez pas respecté la priorité.** vōō nävä pä respektä lá prē·ôrētā.
You cut the corner.	**Vous avez coupé le virage.** vōōzävä kōōpä lə vēräzh.
You were following too closely.	**Vous m'avez collé.** vōō mävä kôlä.
You were going too fast.	**Vous rouliez trop vite.** vōō rōōlyä trō vēt.
You damaged the ...	**Vous avez endommagé ...** vōōzävä äNdômäzhā ...
May I have your name and address, please?	**Donnez-moi votre nom et votre adresse, s'il vous plaît.** dônä-mô·ä vôt'rə nôN ā vôträdres, sēl vōō ple.
May I have your insurance information, please?	**Donnez-moi le nom et le numéro de votre assurance, s'il vous plaît.** dônä-mô·ä lə nôN ā lə nēmärō də vôträsē̄räNs, sēl vōō ple.

78

Here is my name and address.	**Voici mon nom et mon adresse.** vô·äsē môN nôN ä mônädres.

Here is my insurance information.	**Voici le nom et le numéro de mon assurance.** vô·äsē lə nôN ä lə nēmärō də mônäsēräNs.

!	**Remplissez ce constat à l'amiable, s'il vous plaît.** räNplēsā sə kôNstä ä lämē·äb'lə, sēl vōō ple.	Would you fill out this accident form, please?

Would you mind being a witness?	**Vous pouvez servir de témoin?** vōō pōōvā servēr də tāmô·eN?

Do it yourself

3

Could you lend me ..., please?	**Vous pouvez me prêter ..., s'il vous plaît?** vōō pōōvā mə prätā ..., sēl vōō ple?

a bicycle repair kit	**un set de réparation pour vélo** eN set də räpäräsyôN pōōr vālō
a pump	**une pompe à air** ēn pôNp ä er
a ... wrench	**une clef anglaise (numéro ...)** ēn klä äNglez (nēmärō ...)
a screwdriver	**un tournevis** eN tōōrnəvēs
a ... socket wrench	**une clef à douille (numéro ...)** ēn klä ä dōō'ē (nēmärō ...)
a jack	**un cric** eN krēk
a tool kit	**des outils** dāzōōtē
a pair of pliers	**des pinces** dā peNs

79

At the Repair Shop

Where is the nearest garage/... -dealer's garage?	**Où est le garage/le concessionnaire le plus proche?** oō e lə gäräzh/lə kôNsesyôner lə plē prôsh?
My car's (on the road to)	**Ma voiture se trouve (sur la route de) ...** mä vô·ätẹr sə trōōv (sẹr lä rōōt də)
Can you tow it away?	**Vous pouvez la remorquer?** vōō pōōvā lä rəmôrkā?
Would you come with me?	**Vous pouvez venir avec moi?** vōō pōōvā vənẹr ävek mô·ä?
Would you have a look at it?	**Vous pourriez regarder, s'il vous plaît?** vōō pōōryā rəgärdā, sēl vōō ple?
... is broken.	**... est cassé.** ... e käsā.
My car won't start.	**Ma voiture ne démarre pas.** mä vô·ätẹr nə dāmär pä.
The battery is dead.	**La batterie est vide.** lä bätrē e vēd.
The engine *sounds funny/doesn't have any power*.	**Le moteur *fait un bruit bizarre/ne tire pas.*** lə môtẹr *fe eN brē̄·ē̄ bēzär/nə* tēr pä.
Just do the essential repairs, please.	**Ne faites que les réparations stricte-ment nécessaires.** nə fet kə lā räpäräsyôN strēktəmäN näseser.

| Can I still drive it? | **Est-ce que je peux encore rouler avec?** eskə zhə pã äNkôr rōōlä ävek? |
| When will it be ready? | **Elle sera prête quand?** el sərä pret käN? |

Car, Motorbike and Bike

to accelerate	**accélérer** äksālärā
accelerator	**l'accélérateur** *m* läksälärätēr
accident	**l'accident** *m* läksēdäN
– report	**le constat à l'amiable** lə kôNstä ä lämē·äb'lə
air conditioning	**la climatisation** lä klēmätēzäsyôN
air filter	**le filtre à air** lə fēlträler
ambulance	**l'ambulance** *f* läNbēläNs
antifreeze	**l'antigel** *m* läNtēzhel
automatic transmission	**le changement de vitesses automatique** lə shäNzhmäN də vētes ôtômätēk
battery	**la batterie** lä bätrē
bicycle	**la bicyclette** lä bēsēklet
brake	**le frein** lə freN
– fluid	**le liquide de freins** lə lēkēd də freN
– light	**les feux** *m/pl* **de stop** lā fē də stôp
broken	**cassé** käsā
bumper	**le pare-chocs** lə pär-shôk
car	**la voiture** lä vô·ätēr

3

carburetor	**le carburateur** lə kärbērätär
catalytic converter	**le pot catalytique** lə pô kätälētēk
to change	**changer** shäNzhā
– gears	**passer une vitesse** päsā ēn vētes
child seat	**le siège pour enfant** lə syezh pōōr äNfäN
clutch	**l'embrayage** m läNbreyäzh
curve	**le virage** lə vēräzh
dealer's garage	**le concessionnaire** lə kôNsesyôner
distilled water	**l'eau** f **distillée** lō dēstēlā
to drive	**rouler** rōōlā
driver's license	**le permis de conduire** lə permē də kôNdē·ēr
dynamo	**la dynamo** lä dēnämô
emergency brake	**le frein à main** lə freN ä meN
engine	**le moteur** lə môtär
exhaust	**le pot d'échappement** lə pô dāshäpmäN
fan belt	**la courroie** lä kōōrô·ä
fender	**l'aile** f lel
first-aid kit	**la boîte de premiers secours** lä bô·ät də prəmyā səkōōr
four-wheel drive	**le 4×4** lə kät'rə kät'rə
fuse	**le fusible** lə fēsēb'lə
garage	**l'atelier** m **de réparation** lätəlyā də räpäräsyôN
gas	**l'essence** f lesäNs
– station	**la station-service** lä stäsyôN-servēs

gear	**la vitesse** lä vētes
headlights	**le phare** lə fär
helmet	**le casque** lə käsk
high beams	**les feux** *m/pl* **de route** lā fā̄ də rōōt
highway	**l'autoroute** *f* lôtôrōōt
horn	**le klaxon** lə kläksôN
hubcap	**l'enjoliveur** *m* läNzhôlēvär
ignition	**l'allumage** *m* lälēmäzh
– cable	**le fil d'allumage** lə fēl dälēmäzh
injured	**blessé** blesā
innertube	**la chambre à air** lä shäNbräler
insurance	**l'assurance** *f* läsēräNs
interstate road	**la route nationale** lä rōōt näsyônäl
joint	**le joint** lə zhô·eN
kilometer	**le kilomètre** lə kelômet'rə
low beams	**les feux** *m/pl* **de croisement** lā fā̄ də krô·äzmäN
mirror	**le miroir** lə mērô·är
motor home	**le camping-car** lə käNpēng-kär
motorcycle	**la moto** lä mōtō
neutral	**le point mort** lə pô·eN môr
oil	**l'huile** *f* **moteur** lē·ēl môtär
– change	**la vidange** lə vēdäNzh
to park	**se garer** sə gärā
parking garage	**le parking couvert** lə pärkēng kōōver
parking light	**les feux de position** lā fā̄ də pôzēsyôN
parking lot	**le parking** lə pärkēng
parking receipt machine	**l'horodateur** *m* lôrôdätär

3

83

pressure	**la pression des pneus** lä presyôN dā pnā
radiator	**le radiateur** lə rädē·ätār
rear-end collision	**le télescopage** lə täleskôpäzh
registration number	**le numéro d'immatriculation** lə nēmārō dēmätrēkēläsyôN
to rent	**louer** lōō·ā
repair	**la réparation** lä räpäräsyôN
to repair	**réparer** räpärā
right of way	**la priorité** lä prē·ôrētā
seatbelt	**la ceinture *f* de sécurité** lä seNtēr də sākērētā
shock absorbers	**l'amortisseur *m*** lämôrtēsār
spark plug	**la bougie** lä bōōzhē
snow chains	**les chaînes *f/pl* à neige** lā shen ä nezh
spare gas canister	**le bidon de secours** lə bēdôN də səkōōr
spare part	**la pièce de rechange** lä pyes də rəshäNzh
spare tire	**le pneu de secours** lə pnā də səkōōr
starter	**le démarreur** lə dāmärār
state road	**la route secondaire** lä rōōt səkôNder
steering	**la direction** lä dēreksyôN
taillight	**les feux *m/pl* arrière** lā fā äryer
tire	**le pneu** lə pnā
toll	**le péage** lə pā·äzh
– booth	**le péage** lə pā·äzh

– road	**la section à péage** lä seksyôN ä pā·äzh
to tow (away)	**remorquer** rəmôrkā
tow rope	**le câble de remorquage** lə käb'lə də rəmôrkäzh
transmission	**la boîte de vitesses** lä bô·ät də vētes
turn indicator	**le clignotant** lə klēnyôtäN
unleaded	**sans plomb** säN plôN
valve	**la soupape** lä sōōpáp
van	**le minibus** lə mēnēbēs
vehicle registration	**la carte grise** lä kärt grēz
warning sign	**le triangle de signalisation** lə trē·äNg'lə də sēnyälēzäsyôN
water	**l'eau** *f* lō
wheel	**la roue** lä rōōt
windshield wiper blades	**les balais** *m/pl* **d'essuie-glaces** lā bäle desē·ē·gläs
witness	**le témoin** lə tāmô·eN

3

BUS, SUBWAY, TAXI

By Bus and Subway

Where's the nearest subway station?	**Où est la station de métro la plus proche?** ōō e lä stäsyōN də mätrō lä plē prôsh?
Where's *bus/streetcar* stop for ...?	**Où se trouve l'arrêt du *bus/tramway* pour ...?** ōō sə trōōv läre dē *bēs/ trämōō·e* pōōr ...?
Which *bus/subway* goes to ...?	**Quel *bus/métro* va à ...?** kel *bēs/mätrō* vä ä ...?
❗ La ligne ... lä lēn'yə ...	Number...
When is the next *bus/ streetcar* to ...?	**A quelle heure part le prochain *bus/ tramway* pour ...?** äkelär pär lə prôsheN *bēs/trämōō·e* pōōr ...?
When does the last *bus/subway* return?	**A quelle heure revient le dernier *bus/ métro*?** äkelär rəvyeN lə dernyä *bēs/ mätrō*?
Does this *bus/subway* go to ...?	**Est-ce que ce *bus/métro* va à ...?** eskə sə *bēs/mätrō* vä ä ...?
Do I have to transfer to get to ...?	**Pour ..., est-ce que je dois changer?** pōōr ..., eskə zhə dô·ä shäNzhā?
Could you tell me where I have to *get off/transfer*, please?	**Pouvez-vous me dire où je dois *descendre/changer*?** pōōvā-vōō mə dēr ōō zhə dô·ä dāsäNd'rə/shäNzhā?

INFO You can obtain bus tickets at bus stations or major bus stops; otherwise you can purchase them from the bus driver. Don't forget to stamp them in the machine on the bus, otherwise they are not valid.

You can buy tickets for the subway and commuter trains at the window in front of the entrance. In Paris, as well as some other big cities, you can obtain a general ticket for the entire transportation system or for certain parts of it. In addition there are also special tickets for tourists that include the entrance fees to museums, such as the ticket **Paris-Visite**.

Rather than buy individual tickets, it is advisable to purchase a **carnet** (a book of 10 tickets). When you enter the **métro** (subway), you must put your card through the barrier in order to get in. Your ticket is then valid within the **métro** system until you leave it.

Where can I get a ticket?	**Où est-ce qu'on peut acheter les tickets?** ōō eskôN pä äshtā lā tēke?
Are there ...	**Il y a ...** ēlyä ...
day passes?	**des tickets pour la journée?** dā tēke pōōr lä zhōōrnā?
weekly tickets?	**des cartes hebdomadaires?** dā kärt ebdômäder?
books of tickets?	**des carnets?** dā kärne?
I'd like a ticket to ..., please.	**Un ticket pour ..., s'il vous plaît.** eN tēke pōōr ..., sēl vōō ple.

Taxi!

Where can I get a taxi?	**Où est-ce que je peux avoir un taxi?** ō eskə zhə pā āvô-ár eN täksē?

Could you order a taxi for me for tomorrow morning at ... o'clock?	**Vous pourriez me commander un taxi pour demain matin à ... heures?** vōō pōōryä mə kômäNdā eN täksē pōōr dəmeN mäteN ä ... ār?

..., s'il vous plaît. sēl vōō ple.

To the train station	**À la gare** ä lä gär
To the airport	**À l'aéroport** ä lä-ārōpôr
To the ... Hotel	**À l'hôtel ...** ä lōtel ...

How much is it to ...?	**Combien ce sera pour aller à ...?** kôNbyeN sə sərä pōōr älä ä ...?

(In the hotel) I was told it would only cost ... francs.	**On m'a dit (à l'hôtel) que ça ne coûte que ... francs.** ôN mä dē (ä lōtel) kə sä nə kōōt kə ... fräN.

Would you *start/reset* the taxometer, please?	**Mettez votre compteur *en marche/sur zéro*, s'il vous plaît.** metā vôt'rə kôNtār äN märsh/sār zārō, sēl vōō ple.

Could you *wait/stop* here (for a moment), please?	***Attendez/Arrêtez-vous* (un instant) ici, s'il vous plaît.** ätäNdā/ärätā-vōō (eNeNstäN) ēsē, sēl vōō ple.

bus	**le bus** lə bēs
– stop	**l'arrêt** *m* **de bus** läre də bēs
– terminal	**la gare routière** lä gär rōōtyer
to change	**changer** shäNzha
commuter train	**le RER** lə er-ə-er
day pass	**le ticket pour la journée** lə tēke pōōr lä zhōōrnā
departure	**le départ** lə dāpär
direction	**la direction** lä dēreksyôN
driver	**le chauffeur** lə shôfär
to get out	**descendre** dāsäNd'rə
last stop	**le terminus** lə termēnēs
receipt	**le reçu** lə rəsē
schedule	**l'horaire** *m* lôrer
to stamp (a ticket)	**composter** kôNpôstā
stop	**l'arrêt** *m* läre
streetcar	**le tramway** lə trämōō·e
subway	**le métro** lə mātrō
taxi	**le taxi** lə täksē
– stand	**la station de taxis** lä stäsyôN də täksē
ticket	**le ticket** lə tēke
– (vending) machine	**le distributeur automatique de tickets** lə dēstrēbētär ôtômätēk də tēke
weekly ticket	**la carte hebdomadaire** lä kärt ebdômäder

3

HITCHHIKING

I'd like to go to ...

Je voudrais aller à ... zhə vōōdre älä ä ...

Where/Which way are you going?

Vous allez où? vōōzälä ōō?

Can you take me (a part of the way) there?

Vous pouvez m'emmener (un bout de chemin)? vōō pōōvā mämnā (eN bōōdshəmeN)?

? **Où voulez-vous descendre?** ōō vōōlā-vōō däsäNd'rə?

Where do you want to get off?

Could you let me out here, please?

Laissez-moi descendre ici, s'il vous plaît. lesā-mô·ä däsäNdrēsē, sēl vōō ple.

Thanks for the lift.

Merci beaucoup de m'avoir emmené. mersē bōkōō də mävô·är ämnā.

90

Food and Drink

MENU MENU

Potages et soupes *Soups*

bouillabaisse *f* bōōyäbes   (southern French) fish soup

consommé *m* kôNsômä   consommé

potage *m* **parmentier**   potato soup
pôtäzh pärmäNtyä

soupe *f* **à l'oignon**   French onion soup
sōōp ä lônyôN

soupe *f* **de poisson**   fish soup
sōōp də pô-äsôN

Hors-d'œuvre *Appetizers*

avocat *m* **vinaigrette**   avocados in vinaigrette
ävôkä vēnegret

charcuterie *f* shärkē̇trē   cold cut platter

cœurs *m/pl* **d'artichauts**   artichoke hearts
kär därtēshō

crudités *f/pl* **(variées)**   crudités (fresh, raw vegetable
krē̇dētä (väryä)   platter as finger food)

huîtres *f/pl* ē̇·ēt'rə   oysters

olives *f/pl* ôlēv   olives

pâté *m* pätä   (liver) pâté

   – de campagne   coarse (liver) pâté
   də käNpän'yə

pissenlits *m/pl* **au lard**   dandelion green salad with
pēsäNlē ō lär   bacon

rillettes (de tours) *f/pl*   (pork) pâté
rēyet (də tōōr)

salade *f* säläd — salad
  - **– composée** kôNpôzā — chef salad
  - **– mixte** mēkst — mixed salad
  - **– niçoise** nēsô·äz — green salad with eggs, tomatoes, sardines, olives, and capers

saumon *m* **fumé** sōmôN fēmā — smoked salmon

terrine *f* **de canard** — duck pâté
terēn də känär

Entrées Starters

bouchées *f/pl* **à la reine** — vol au vents
bōōshā ä lä ren

crêpes *f/pl* krep — crêpes

croque-monsieur *m* — toasted ham-and-cheese sand-
krôk-məsyā — wich

escargots *m/pl* eskärgō — snails

omelette *f* **aux champignons** — mushroom omelette
ômlet ō shäNpēnyôN

quiche *f* **lorraine** kēsh lôren — quiche lorraine (bacon and cheese quiche)

tarte *f* **à l'oignon** tärt ä lônyôN — onion tart

Viandes Meat dishes

agneau *m* änyō — lamb

bœuf *m* bāf — beef

lièvre *m* lēyev'rə — hare

mouton *m* mōōtôN — mutton

4

93

porc *m* pôr	pork
veau *m* vō	veal
andouillette *f* äNdōōyet	tripe sausage
bifteck *m* bēftek	steak
bœuf *m* **bourguignon** bäf bōōrgēnyôN	beef in red wine
bœuf *m* **à la mode** bäf ä lä môd	pot roast
boudin *m* bōōdeN	blood sausage
cassoulet *m* käsōōle	casserole of navy beans, goose, and other meats
côte *f* kōt	chop
escalope *f* **de veau** eskälôp də vō	veal cutlet
filet *m* **de bœuf** fēle də bäf	filet of beef
gigot *m* **d'agneau** zhēgō dänyō	leg of lamb
grillade *f* grēyäd	grilled meat platter
hachis *m* äshē	meat loaf
jarret *m* **de veau** zhäre də vō	knuckle of veal
quenelles *f/pl* kənel	meat or fish dumplings
ris *m* **de veau** rē də vō	veal sweetbreads
rôti *m* rōtē	roast
sauté *m* **de veau** sôtā də vō	veal stew
selle *f* **d'agneau** sel dänyō	rack of lamb
steak *m* stek	steak
– au poivre ō pô·âv'rə	pepper –
– haché äshā	Salisbury –
tournedos *m* tōōrnədō	fillet steak
tripes *f/pl* trēp	tripe

Volaille *Poultry*

blanc *m* **de poulet**
bläN də pōōle
chicken breast

canard *m* **à l'orange**
känär ä lôräNzh
duck with orange sauce

confit *m* **de canard**
kôNfē də känär
duck preserved in its own fat

coq *m* **au vin** kôkōveN
chicken in wine sauce

dinde *f* deNd
turkey

pintade *f* peNtäd
guinea fowl

poulet *m* **rôti** pōōle rōtē
roast chicken

Poissons *Fish*

aiglefin *m* āgləfeN
haddock

anguille *f* äNgē'yə
eel

brochet *m* brôshe
pike

cabillaud *m* käbēyō
cod

calmar *m* **frit** kälmär frē
deep-fried squid

carpe *f* kärp
carp

colin *m* kôleN
hake

friture *f* frētēr
mixed deep-fried fish

lotte *f* lôt
monkfish

morue *f* môrē
dried cod

rouget *m* rōōzhe
perch

saumon *m* sōmôN
salmon

sole *f* sôl
sole

thon *m* tôN
tuna

truite *f* **au bleu** trē-ēt ō blə
poached trout

4

Coquillages et crustacés — *Seafood*

coquilles *f/pl* **Saint-Jacques** scallops
kôkē'yə seN-zhäk

crabes *m/pl* kräb crabs

crevettes *f/pl* krəvet shrimps

écrevisses *f/pl* ākrəvēs freshwater crawfishes

huîtres *f/pl* ē-ēt'rə oysters

langouste *f* läNgōōst crawfish, spiny lobster

langoustines *f/pl* läNgōōstēn Dublin bay prawns

moules *f/pl* mōōl mussels

plateau *m* **de fruits de mer** seafood platter
plätō də frē-ē də mer

Légumes — *Vegetables*

artichauts *m/pl* ärtēshō artichokes

asperges *f/pl* äsperzh asparagus

aubergines *f/pl* ōberzhēn eggplants

carottes *f/pl* kärōt carrots

champignons *m/pl* mushrooms
shäNpēnyôN

chou *m* shōō cabbage

  – de Bruxelles də brēsel Brussels sprouts

  – -fleur flār cauliflower

  – rouge rōōzh red cabbage

choucroute *f* shōōkrōōt sauerkraut

courgettes *f/pl* kōōrzhet zucchinis

épinards *m/pl* āpēnär spinach

endives *f/pl* äNdēv Belgian endive

fenouil *m* fənōō'ē	fennel
haricots *m/pl* ärēkō	beans
macédoine *f* **de légumes**	mixed vegetables
mäsädô·än də lāgēm	
navets *m/pl* näve	turnips
petits pois *m/pl* pətē pô·ä	peas
poivron *m* pô·ävrôN	bell pepper
ratatouille *f* rätätōō'ē	vegetable stew of tomatoes, peppers, zucchini, and eggplant

Comment le désirez-vous? How would you like it?

bien cuit byeN kē̠·ē	well done
(fait) maison (fe) māzôN	homemade
farci färsē	stuffed
fumé fēmā	smoked
gratiné grätēnā	au gratin
rôti rōtē	roasted

Garnitures Vegetables and side dishes

4

gratin *m* **dauphinois**	potatoes au gratin
gräteN dōfēnô·ä	
pâtes *f/pl* pät	pasta
pommes *f/pl* **de terre**	potatoes
pôm də ter	
– **frites** frēt	French fries
– **sautées** sōtā	fried potatoes
riz *m* rē	rice

Fromages Cheese

bleu *m* blā — blue cheese
fromage *m* frômäzh — cheese
   – au lait cru ō le krē — cheese made from un-pasteurized milk
   – de brebis də brəbē — feta cheese
   – de chèvre də shev'rə — goat's cheese
plateau *m* **de fromages** plätō də frômäzh — cheese platter

Desserts Desserts

beignets *m/pl* **aux pommes** benye ō pôm — fried apple rings
coupe *f* **maison** kōōp mezôN — house ice-cream sundae
crème *f* **caramel** krem kärämel — crème caramel
flan *m* fläN — baked egg custard
glace *f* gläs — ice cream
   – à la fraise ä lä frez — strawberry –
   – à la vanille ä lä vänē'yə — vanilla –
   – au chocolat ō shôkôlä — chocolate –
île *f* **flottante** ēl flôtäNt — ice-cream on vanilla sauce
macédoine *f* **de fruits** mäsādô-än də frē-ē — fruit salad
meringue *f* məreNg — meringue
parfait *m* pärfe — ice-cream parfait

98

Fruits *Fruit*

fraises *f/pl* frez — strawberries
framboises *f/pl* fräNbô-äz — raspberries
melon *m* məlóN — melon
pastèque *f* pästek — watermelon
pêche *f* pesh — peach
poire *f* pô-är — pear
pomme *f* pôm — apple
raisins *m/pl* rezeN — grapes

Gâteaux et pâtisseries *Cake*

biscuit *m* **roulé** — Swiss roll
bēskē·ē rōōlā
cake *m* kek — fruit cake
chausson *m* **aux pommes** — apple Danish
shôsôN ō pôm
chou *m* **à la crème** — cream puff
shōō ä lä krem
éclair *m* äkler — éclair
 – au café ō käfā — coffee –
mille-feuille *m* mēl-fā'ē — napoleon
profiteroles *f/pl* prôfētərôl — small cream puffs
tarte *f* tärt — tart
 – aux pommes ō pôm — apple –
 – Tatin täteN — caramelized apple –
tartelette *f* **aux fraises** — small strawberry tarts
tärtəlet ō frez

BOISSONS BEVERAGES

Apéritifs   aperitifs

kir *m* kēr   kir
porto *m* pôrtō   port
pastis *m* pästēs   anise liqueur

Vins   Wine

vin *m* veN   wine
   – **blanc** bläN   white –
   – **rouge** rōōzh   red –
   – **rosé** rōzā   rosé
   – **d'appellation contrôlée**   vintage –
     däpeläsyôN kôNtrôlā
   – **mousseux** mōōsā   sparkling –
champagne *m* shäNpän'yə   champagne
brut brē   dry
(demi-)sec (dəmē) sek   (medium) dry
doux dōō   sweet

Autres boissons alcoolisées   Other alcoholic drinks

bière *f* byer   beer
   – **sans alcool** säN älkôl   nonalcoholic –
   – **brune** brēn   ale
   – **blonde** blôNd   lager
   – **pression** presyôN   draft beer
bitter *m* bēter   bitters

calvados *m* kälvädôs	applejack
cassis *m* käsēs	red-currant liqueur
digestif *m* dēzhestēf	digestive schnapps

Boissons non alcoolisées   *Non-alcoholic drinks*

citron *m* **pressé** sētrôN presā	freshly squeezed lemon juice
eau *f* **minérale** ō mēnäräl	mineral water
– gazeuse gázāz	carbonated –
– non gazeuse nôN gázāz	noncarbonated –
jus *m* zhē	juice
– de pomme də pôm	apple –
– d'orange dôräNzh	orange –
– de tomate də tômät	tomato –
limonade *f* lēmônäd	(fizzy) lemonade
menthe *f* mäNt	peppermint syrup with mineral water

Boissons chaudes   *Hot drinks*

café *m* käfā	coffee
– express ekspres	espresso
– au lait ō le	– with hot milk
– crème krem	– with frothed milk
chocolat *m* **chaud** shôkôlä shō	hot chocolate
infusion *f* eNfēzyôN	herbal tea
thé *m* tā	tea
– au citron ō sētrôN	– with lemon

4

INFORMATION

Where is ... around here?	**Où y a-t-il ici ...** ōō yätēl ...
a good restaurant	**un bon restaurant?** eN bôN restôrâN?
an inexpensive restaurant	**un restaurant pas trop cher?** eN restôrâN pä trō sher?
a restaurant typical for this area	**un restaurant typique?** eN restôrâN tēpēk?
a bar	**un bistrot?** eN bēstrō?
a café	**un salon de thé?** eN sälôN də tā?

INFO One visits the **café** primarily to get something to drink; they might also have sandwiches there, **croque-monsieur** (toasted ham and cheese) or **croque-madame** (toasted ham and cheese with pineapple). In the morning you can also get a French breakfast there.

In the **café-bar** there might only be a few tables. Most people will be standing at the bar. If cigarettes are also sold there, it will be called a **café-bar-tabac**, indicated by a large, red cigar hanging on the door.

In the **café-restaurant** you can get something to drink and/or eat. The service and decor are unembellished, the food and drink inexpensive.

A **bistro** is a smaller café, usually with an interesting atmosphere. In Paris you can sample different wines at the **bistros à vin**. They usually also offer a few (regional) dishes such as **steak**, **bœuf bourguignon**, etc., so that you don't have to drink on an empty stomach.

| A table for ..., please. | **Une table pour ... personnes, s'il vous plaît.** ēn täb'lə pōōr ... persôN, sēl vōō ple. |
| May I have this seat? | **Est-ce que cette place est libre?** eske set pläs e lēb'rə? |

INFO At the **café** you may sit down where there is space available, even at tables where other people are sitting. This is not a good idea at a **restaurant**: you should wait until you are shown to a table.

| Do you have a high-chair? | **Avez-vous une chaise haute pour enfants?** ävā-vōō ēn shez ōt pōōr äNfäN? |
| Excuse me, where are the restrooms? | **Pardon, où sont les toilettes?** pärdôN, ōō sôN lā tô·älet? |

! **Par ici.** pär ēsē.   Down here.

WAITER!

| May I see a menu, please? | **La carte, s'il vous plaît.** lä kärt, sēl vōō ple. |

INFO In France you can call the waiter by saying **Monsieur** məsyā, and call the waitress by saying **Madame** mädäm or **Mademoiselle** mädmô·äzel.

4

I'd like something to eat.	**Je voudrais manger.** zhə vōōdre mäNzhā.	

I'd just like something small to eat. **Je voudrais seulement manger un petit quelque chose.** zhə vōōdre sälmäN mäNzhā eN pətē kelkə shōz.

Are you still serving hot meals? **Est-ce qu'on peut encore avoir quelque chose de chaud à manger?** eskôN pā äNkôr ävô·är kelkə shōz də shō ä mäNzhā?

I just want something to drink. **Je voudrais seulement boire quelque chose.** zhə vōōdre sälmäN bô·är kelkə shōz.

? **Que désirez-vous boire?** kə dāzērā-vōō bô·är? — What would you like to drink?

I'd like ..., please. **Je voudrais ...** zhə vōōdre ...

a quarter of a liter of red wine.	**un quart de vin rouge.** eN kär də veN rōōzh.
a carafe of water	**une carafe d'eau.** ēn käräf dō.
a bottle of mineral water	**une bouteille d'eau minérale.** ēn bōōte'ē dō mēnäräl.

Can I get a carafe of wine? **Avez-vous aussi du vin en carafe?** ävā-vōō ôsē dḛ veN äN käräf?

? **Que désirez-vous manger?** kə dāzērā-vōō mäNzhā? — What would you like to eat?

I'd like ...	**Je voudrais ...** zhǝ vōōdre ...
the meal for ... francs.	**le menu à ... francs.** lǝ mǝnē ä ... fräN.
a serving of ...	**une portion de ...** ēn pôrsyôN dǝ ...
Do you have ...?	**Avez-vous ...?** ävā-vōō ...?
What would you recommend?	**Que me recommandez-vous?** kǝ mǝ rǝkômäNdā-vōō?

! **Je vous recommande ...** zhǝ vōō rǝkômäNd ...	I can recommend ...

What is the special of the day?	**Quel est le plat du jour?** kel e lǝ plä dē zhōōr?
What are the local specialties?	**Quelles sont les spécialités de la région?** kel sôN lā spāsyälētā dǝ lä räzhē-ôN?
Do you have children's portions?	**Avez-vous un menu enfants?** ävā-vōō eN mǝnē äNfäN?
Do you have ...	**Avez-vous ...** ävā-vōō ...
vegetarian dishes?	**de la cuisine végétarienne?** dǝ lä kē-ēzēn vāzhätäryen?
food suitable for diabetics?	**des plats pour diabétiques?** dā plä pōōr dē-äbätēk?
special diet meals?	**des plats de régime?** dā plä dǝ rāzhēm?

4

| Does that have ... in it? | **Est-ce qu'il y a ... dans ce plat? Je n'ai** |
| I'm not allowed to eat that. | **pas le droit d'en manger.** eskēlyä ... däN sə plä? zhə ne pä lə drô·ä däN mäNzhā. |

| Is there garlic in that? | **Est-ce qu'il y a de l'ail dedans?** eskēlyä də lä'ē dədäN? |

? **Comme** *entrée/dessert,* **qu'est-ce que vous prenez?** kôm äNtrā/ dāser, keskə vōō prənā?   What would you like for *an appetizer/ dessert?*

| Thanks, but I'd rather not have *an appetizer/ any dessert.* | **Merci, je ne prends pas** *d'entrée/de dessert.* mersē, zhə nə präN pä däNtrā/də dāser. |

INFO The French end a good meal with a **plateau de fromages** plätō də frômäzh (cheese platter). There are usually 4 to 5 kinds of cheese on the platter; however, it is considered impolite to sample more than 2 or 3 of them.

| Could I have ... instead of ...? | **Est-ce que je pourrais avoir ... au lieu de ...?** eskə zhə pōōre ävô·är ... ō lēyä də ...? |

| Could you bring me another ..., please? | **Apportez moi encore ..., s'il vous plaît.** äpôrtā mô·ä äNkôr ..., sēl vōō ple. |

INFO Bread – **pain** – is included in the price of meals, and French waiters customarily refill the bread basket as soon as it is empty.

?	**Comment désirez-vous votre steak?** kômäN dāzērā-vōō vôt'rə stek?	How would you like your steak?

Rare.	**Saignant.** senyäN.	
Medium.	**A point.** ä pô·eN.	
Well done.	**Bien cuit.** byeN kē·ē.	

INFO In a restaurant you will usually get a complementary carafe of water for your table. Many people in France, however, have begun drinking mineral water, with the result that waiters do not always automatically bring plain water to the tables. Do not hesitate to ask for **une carafe d'eau** ēn käräf dō (a pitcher of water).

COMPLAINTS

I didn't order this. I wanted ...	**Ce n'est pas ce que j'ai commandé. Je voulais ...** sə ne pä səkə zhā kômäNdā. zhə vōōle ...
The ... *is/are* missing.	**Ici, il manque encore ...** ēsē, ēl mäNk äNkôr ...
The food is ...	**C'est ...** se ...
cold.	**trop froid.** trō frô·ä..
too salty.	**trop salé.** trō sälā.
too greasy.	**trop gras.** trō grä..

4

107

This is no longer fresh.	**Ce n'est plus très frais.**
	sə ne plē tre fre.
The meat hasn't been cooked enough.	**La viande n'est pas assez cuite.**
	lä vyäNd n'est pä päzäsā kē-ēt.
Would you take it back, please?	**Remportez cela, s'il vous plaît.**
	räNpôrtā səlä, sēl vōō ple.

THE CHECK, PLEASE.

? **Vous êtes satisfaits?**
vōōzet sätēsfe?

Did you enjoy your meal?

It was very nice, thank you.	**Merci, c'était très bon.**
	mersē, säte tre bôN.
Could I have the check, please?	**L'addition, s'il vous plaît.**
	lädēsyôN, sēl vōō ple.
I'd like a receipt.	**Je voudrais une facture.**
	zhə vōōdre ēn fäktēr.

INFO Waiters will not continually visit your table to ask if you want anything else or if everything is all right. They will also not bring the check when you have finished your meal until you ask for it. If you wish to have separate checks, you must tell the waiter that **"Nous voudrions payer séparément"** nōō vōōdrēôN päyā säpärämäN. The check will be brought discreetly on a small plate.

May I treat you?	**Je peux t'inviter?** zhə pə teNvētā?

You're my guest today.	**Aujourd'hui, c'est moi qui vous invite.** ōzhōōrdvē, se mô·ä kē vōōzeNvēt.
I think there must be some mistake here.	**A mon avis, il y a une erreur.** ä mônävē, ēlyä ēn erär.
Will you please add it up again?	**Vous pourriez me refaire le compte, s'il vous plaît?** vōō pōōryā mə rəfer lə kôNt, sēl vōō ple?
We didn't order this.	**Nous n'avions pas commandé cela.** nōō nävyôN pä kômäNdä səlä.
Thank you very much.	**Merci beaucoup.** mersē bōkōō.

DINING WITH FRIENDS

Enjoy your meal!	**Bon appétit!** bônäpātē!
Your health!	**A votre/ta santé!** ä vôt' rə/tä säNtā!
Cheers!	**Tchin-tchin!** tshēn-tshēn!

? **Vous aimez/tu aimes ça?** How do you like it?
vōōzāmā/tⓔ em sä?

| It's very good, thank you. | **Merci, c'est très bon.** mersē, se tre bôN. |
| That's absolutely delicious. | **C'est absolument délicieux.** setäbsôlⓔmäN dālēsyä. |

? **Vous en voulez?/Tu en veux?** Would you like some
vōōzäN vōōlā?/tⓔ äN vä? of this?

109

! **C'est une spécialité française.** | This is a French spe-
setēn spāsyälētā fränsez. | ciality.

? **Encore un peu de ...?** | Would you like some
äNkôr eN pā də ...? | more ...?

Yes, please. | **Oui, volontiers.** ōō·ē, vôlôNtyā.

No, thanks, I'm fine | **Pas pour l'instant, merci.**
for the moment. | pä pōōr leNstäN, mersē.

No, thank you, I'm | **Je n'ai plus faim, merci.**
full. | zhe ne plē feN, mersē.

What's that? | **Qu'est-ce que c'est?** keskə se?

INFO If you order **un café** in a **café**, you will receive a
small cup of coffee without milk. You can also get
un café crème, or **un crème** for short, which is a cup of coffee
with frothy milk. If you would like a large cup, ask for **un grand
crème**.

Would you pass me | **Vous pourriez/Tu pourrais me passer**
the ..., please? | **..., s'il vous/te plaît?** vōō pōōryā/tē
pōōre mə päsā ..., sēl vōō/tə ple?

Do you mind if I | **Ça vous/te dérange si je fume?**
smoke? | sä vōō/tə däräNzh se zhə fēm?

Thank you for inviting | **Merci pour l'invitation.**
me/us. | mersē pōōr leNvētäsyôN.

It was wonderful. | **C'était excellent.** sāte ekseläN.

➡ *Please; Thank you (p. 26)*

Food and drink

alcohol	**l'alcool** *m* lälkôl
appetizer	**l'entrée** *f*, **le hors-d'œuvre** läNtrā, lə ôr-dặv'rə
artificial sweetener	**la saccharine** lä säkärēn
ashtray	**le cendrier** lə säNdrē·ā
available	**libre** lēb'rə
bar	**le bistrot** lə bēstrō
beer	**la bière** lä byär
bottle	**la bouteille** lä bōōte'ē
bread	**le pain** lə peN
– roll	**le petit pain** lə pətē peN
white –	**le pain blanc** lə peN bläN
breakfast	**le petit déjeuner** lə pətē dāzhāṇā
to bring	**apporter** äpôrtā
butter	**le beurre** lə bār
cake	**le gâteau** lə gätō
carafe	**la carafe** lä käräf
chair	**la chaise** lä shez
chamomile tea	**la camomille** lä kämōmē'yə
cheese	**le fromage** lə frômäzh
cocoa	**le cacao** lə käkä·ō
coffee	**le café** lə käfā
black –	**le café noir** lə käfā nô·är
decaffeinated –	**le café décaféiné** lə käfā dākäfā·ēnā
– with hot milk	**le café au lait** lə käfā ō le
cold	**froid** frô·ä
– cuts	**la charcuterie** lä shärkạtrē

4

111

cream	**la chantilly** lä shäNtēyē
crisp bread	**le pain croustillant** lə peN krōōstēyäN
cup	**la tasse** lä täs
dessert	**le dessert** lə däser
diabetic *(person)*	**le diabétique** lə dē·ábätēk
diabetic *(special food)*	**diabétique** dē·ábätēk
diet	**le régime** lə räzhēm
dinner	**le dîner** lə dēnä
dish	**le plat** *m* lə plä
drink	**la boisson** lä bô·äsôN
to drink	**boire** bô·är
drinks menu	**la carte des boissons** lä kärt dā bô·äsôN
to eat	**manger** mäNzhä
egg	**l'œuf** *m, pl:* **les œufs** läf, *pl:* läzə
fried –	**l'œuf** *m* **au plat** läf ō plä
hard-boiled –	**l'œuf** *m* **dur** läf dēr
scrambled –	**l'œuf** *m* **brouillé** läf brōōyä
soft-boiled –	**l'œuf** *m* **à la coque** läf á lä kôk
excellent	**excellent** ekseläN
fat	**le gras** lə grä
fatty	**gras** grä
fish	**le poisson** lə pô·äsôN
fork	**la fourchette** lä fōōrshet
fresh	**frais,** *f:* **fraîche** fre, *f:* fresh
fresh, raw vegetable platter *(finger food)*	**les crudités** *f/pl* lā krēdētä

fruit	**les fruits** *m/pl* lā frē̇·ē̇
to be full	**ne plus avoir faim** nə plēzävô·är feN
garlic	**l'ail** *m* lä'ē̇
glass	**le verre** lə ver
grease	**le gras** lə grä
greasy	**gras** grä
ham	**le jambon** lə zhäNbôN
hamburger	**le hamburger** lə äNbērgär
hard	**dur** dēr
to have breakfast	**prendre le petit déjeuner** präNd'rə lə pətē dāzhānā
herbs	**les fines herbes** *f/pl* lā fēn erb
homemade	**(fait) maison** (fe) mezôN
honey	**le miel** lə myel
hot *(temperature)*	**chaud** shō
hot *(spicy)*	**épicé** āpēsā
to be hungry	**avoir faim** ävô·är feN
ice (cube)	**le glaçon** lə gläsôN
ice cream	**la glace** lä gläs
to invite	**inviter** eNvētā
jam	**la confiture** lä kôNfētēr
ketchup	**le ketchup** lə ketshäp
knife	**le couteau** lə kōōtō
lean	**maigre** meg'rə
light food	**la cuisine diététique** lä kē̇·ēzēn dē̇·ātātēk
lunch	**le déjeuner** lə dāzhānā

4

main course	**le plat de résistance**
	lə plä də räzēstäNs
margarine	**la margarine** lä märgärēn
mayonnaise	**la mayonnaise** lä mäyônez
meal	**le repas** lə rəpä
meat	**la viande** lä vyäNd
menu	**la carte** lä kärt
milk	**le lait** lə le
mineral water	**l'eau** f **minérale** lō mēnäräl
carbonated –	**l'eau** f **gazeuse** lō gäzə̄z
non-carbonated –	**l'eau** f **plate** lō plät
mushrooms	**les champignons** m/pl lā shäNpēnyôN
mustard	**la moutarde** lä mōōtärd
napkin	**la serviette** lä servyet
non-alcoholic	**sans alcool** säNsälkôl
oil	**l'huile** f lē·ēl
olive –	**l'huile** f **d'olive** lē·ēl dôlēv
onion	**l'oignon** m lônyôN
order	**la commande** lä kômäNd
to order	**commander** kômäNdā
pastries	**les gâteaux** m/pl **secs** lā gätō sek
to pay	**payer** päyā
pepper	**le poivre** lə pô·äv'rə
peppermint tea	**l'infusion** f **de menthe**
	leNfē̄zyôN də mäNt
piece	**le morceau** lə môrsō
pizza	**la pizza** lä pētsä
place setting	**le couvert** lə kōōver
plate	**l'assiette** f läsyet

portion	**la portion** lä pôrsyôN
pumpernickel	**le pain bis** lə peN bē
to reserve	**réserver** räzervä
restaurant	**le restaurant** lə restôräN
rest room	**les toilettes** *f/pl* lā tô·älet
salad	**la salade** lä säläd
salt	**le sel** lə sel
sandwich	**le sandwich** lə säNdōō·ē(t)sh
sauce	**la sauce** lä sōs
seasoned	**assaisonné** äsesônā
seat	**la place** lä pläs
service	**le service** lə servēs
set menu	**le menu** lə mənē
slice	**la tranche** lä träNsh
soft	**tendre** täNd'rə
soup	**le potage** lə pôtäzh
sour	**aigre** āg'rə
special of the day	**le plat du jour** lə plä dē zhōōr
speciality	**la spécialité** lä späsyälētā
spice	**l'épice** *f* lāpēs
spoon	**la cuillère** lä kē·eyer
straw *(for drinks)*	**la paille** lä pä'yə
sugar	**le sucre** lə sēk'rə
sweet	**sucré** sēkrā
table	**la table** lä täb'lə
tea	**le thé** lə tā
fruit –	**l'infusion** *f* **fruitée** leNfēzyôN frē·ētā
herbal –	**l'infusion** *f* leNfēzyôN

4

to be thirsty	**avoir soif** ävô·är sô·äf
tip	**le pourboire** lə pōōrbô·är
toast	**le toast** lə tōst
vegetables	**les légumes** *m/pl* lā lāgēm
vegetarian	**végétarien** vāzhätäryeN
vinegar	**le vinaigre** lə vēnāg'rə
waiter	**le garçon** lə gärsôN
waitress	**la serveuse** lä servāz
water	**l'eau** *f* lō
wine	**le vin** lə veN
zwieback	**les biscottes** *f/pl* lā bēskôt

 Food (p. 142)

Sightseeing

INFORMATION

Where is the tourist-information office?	**Où se trouve l'office du tourisme?**
	ōō sə trōōv lôfēs dē tōōrēsm?
May I have ...	**Je voudrais ...** zhə vōōdre ...
a list of hotels?	**une liste des hôtels.**
	ēn lēst dāzōtel.
a map of the area?	**un plan des environs.**
	eN pläN dāzäNvērôN.
a street map?	**un plan de la ville.**
	eN pläN də lä vēl.
a subway schedule?	**un plan du métro.**
	eN pläN dē mätrō.
a schedule of events?	**un calendrier des manifestations.**
	eN käläNdrē-ā dā mänēfestäsyôN.
Do you have any brochures in English?	**Est-ce que vous avez aussi des prospectus en anglais?** eskə vōōzävä ôsē dā prôspektēs änäNgle?
Could you reserve a room for me?	**Est-ce que vous pouvez me réserver une chambre?** eskə vōō pōōvä mə rāzervä ēn shäNb'rə?

INFO In many areas and cities popular with tourists, you will find a **petit train touristique**, a little train with open cars that travels through the streets instead of on tracks. Points of interest will be announced over the loudspeaker.

Are there *sightseeing tours/guided walking tours* of the city?	**Est-ce qu'il y a des *tours de ville guidés/visites guidées de la ville*?** eskēlyā dā fōōr də vēl gēdā/vēzēt gēdā də lä vēl?
How much does the sightseeing tour cost?	**Combien coûte le tour de ville guidé?** kôNbyeN kōōt lə tōōr də vēl gēdā?
How long does the walking tour last?	**Combien de temps dure la visite guidée de la ville?** kôNbyeN də täN dēr lä vēzēt gēdā də lä vēl?
I'd like *a ticket/two tickets* for the sightseeing tour, please.	***Un billet/Deux billets*, s'il vous plaît, pour le tour de ville guidé.** eN bēye/də bēye, sēl vōō ple, pōōr lə tōōr de vēl gēdā.

INFO In Paris you can take a trip on the **bateaux-mouches** and see the city from these sightseeing boats on the Seine. They dock at Pont Neuf, Pont de l'Alma, and the Pont d'Iéna under the Eiffel Tower.

I'd like to visit ...	**Je voudrais visiter ...** zhə vōōdre vēzētā ...
When is ... open?	**Quelles sont les heures d'ouverture de ...?** kel sôN lāzär dōōvertēr də ...?

5

Please reserve *a place/two places* on tomorrow's excursion for *me/us*.	*Une place/Deux places* **pour l'excursion de demain à ..., s'il vous plaît.** ēn pläs/dœ̄ pläs pōōr leksē̄rsyôN də dəmeN ä ..., sēl vōō ple.
Where/When do we meet?	*Quand/Où* **est-ce que nous nous rencontrons?** käN/ōō eskə nōō nōō räNkôNtrôN?
Is lunch included in the price?	**Est-ce que le déjeuner est inclus dans le prix?** eskə lə dāzhœ̄nā eteNklē̄ däN lə prē?
Will we also be visiting ...?	**Est-ce que nous allons aussi visiter ...?** eskə nōōzälôN ôsē vēzētā ...?
Will we also have some free time?	**Est-ce que nous avons du temps libre à notre disposition?** eskə nōōzävôN dē̄ täN lēbrə nôt'rə dēspôzēsyôN?
When will it start?	**Nous partons à quelle heure?** nōō pärtôN ä kelēr?
When do we get back?	**Nous rentrons à quelle heure?** nōō räNtrôN ä kelēr?

➡️ *Accommodation (p. 36),*
Bus, Subway, Taxi (p. 86),
On the Way (p. 54)

SIGHTSEEING, EXCURSIONS

When is ... open?	**Quelles sont les heures d'ouverture de ...?** kel sôN lāzär dövertēr də ...?
How long is ... open?	**... ♂ est ouvert/♀ est ouverte jusqu'à quelle heure?** ... ♂ etōōver/♀ etōōvert zhēskä kelǟr?
What does it cost to get in?	**Combien coûte l'entrée?** kôNbyeN kōōt läNtrā?
How much does the guided tour cost?	**Combien coûte la visite guidée?** kônbyeN kōōt lä vēzēt gēdā?
Is there a discount for ...	**Est-ce qu'il y a des réductions pour ...** eskēlyä dā rādēksyôN pōōr ...
families?	**les familles?** lä fämē'ē?
groups?	**les groupes?** lä grōōp?
children?	**les enfants?** läzäNfäN?
senior citizens?	**les personnes du troisième âge?** lä persôn dē trô·äzyem äzh?
students?	**les étudiants?** läzätēdyäN?

? **Vous avez une pièce d'identité sur vous?** vōōzävā ēn pyes dēdäNtētä sēr vōō? — Do you have *some ID/your passport* with you?

Do you also have tours in English?	**Est-ce qu'il y a aussi des visites guidées en anglais?** eskēlyä ôsē dā vēzēt gēdā änäNgle?

5

121

When does the tour begin?	**A quelle heure commence la visite?** äkelär kômäNs lä vēzēt?
One ticket/Two tickets, please.	*Un billet/Deux billets*, s'il vous plaît. eN bēye/dₑ bēye, sēl vōō ple.
Two adults and two children, please.	**Deux adultes, deux enfants, s'il vous plaît.** dₐzädₑlt, dₐzäNfäN, sēl vōō ple.

INFO If you are interested in learning about France's history in an entertaining manner, try to attend a performance of the **Spectacle Son et Lumière**, a narrated slide-show. These presentations are frequently displayed in the castles along the Loire.

Are you allowed to *take pictures/make a video*?	**Est-ce qu'on a le droit de *prendre des photos/filmer*?** eskônä lₑ drô·ä dₑ präNd'rₑ dā fōtō/fēlmä?
What *building/monument* is that?	**Qu'est-ce que c'est que *cet édifice/ce monument*?** keskₑ se kₑ set ādēfēs/sₑ mônₑmäN?
Do you have a *catalog/guide*?	**Vous avez un *catalogue/guide*?** vōōzävä eN kätälôg/gēd?
Do you have a ... of that picture?	**Vous avez une reproduction de ce tableau en ...** vōōzävä ₑn rₑprôdₑksyôN dₑ sₑ täblō äN ...
poster	**poster?** pôster?
postcard	**carte postale?** kärt pôstäl?
slide	**diapositive?** dyäpôsētēv?

abbey	**l'abbaye** *f* läbāē
abstract	**abstrait** äbstre
altar	**l'autel** *m* lōtel
amphitheater	**l'amphithéâtre** *m* läNfētā·ät'rə
antique	**antique** äNtēk
aqueduct	**l'aqueduc** *m* läkdēk
arch	**l'arc** *m* lärk
archeological find	**les vestiges** *m/pl* **archéologiques** lā vestēzh ärkā·ôlôzhēk
archeology	**l'archéologie** *f* lärkā·ôlôzhē
architect	**l'architecte** *m, f* lärshētekt
architecture	**l'architecture** *f* lärshētektēr
arena	**les arènes** *f/pl* läzären
art	**l'art** *m* lär
– collection	**la collection de peintures** lä kôleksyôN də peNtēr
artist	**l'artiste** *m, f* lärtēst
baroque	**baroque** bärôk
basilica	**la basilique** lä bäzēlēk
bell	**la cloche** lä klôsh
bird sanctuary	**la réserve ornithologique** lä rāzerv ôrnētôlôzhēk
botanical gardens	**le jardin botanique** lə zhärdeN bôtänēk
bridge	**le pont** le pôN
brochure	**le prospectus** lə prospektēs
building	**l'édifice** *m* lādēfēs
bust	**le buste** lə bēst

5

123

cable car	**le téléphérique** lə tālāfārēk
canyon	**les gorges** f/pl lā gôrzh
capital *(of a column)*	**le chapiteau** lə shäpētō
castle	**le château** lə shätō
catacombs	**les catacombes** f/pl lā kätäkôNb
catalog	**le catalogue** lə kätälôg
cathedral	**la cathédrale** lä kätādräl
Catholic	**catholique** kätôlēk
cave	**la grotte** lä grôt
ceiling	**le plafond** lə pläfôN
Celtic	**celtique** seltēk
cemetery	**le cimetière** lə sēmtyer
central nave	**la nef centrale** lä nef säNträl
century	**le siècle** lə syek'lə
ceramics	**la céramique** lä särämēk
chair lift	**le télésiège** lə tālāsyezh
chamber of commerce	**le syndicat d'initiative** lə seNdēkä dēnēsyätēv
chapel	**la chapelle** lä shäpel
chimes	**le carillon** lə kärēyôN
choir	**le chœur** lə kār
church	**l'église** f lāglēz
– service	**l'office** m **religieux** lôfēs rəlēzhyā
– steeple	**le clocher** lə klôshā
– windows	**les vitraux** m/pl lā vētrō
city	**la ville** lä vēl
city center	**le centre ville** lə säNt'rə vēl
– district	**le quartier** lə kärtyā
– gate	**la porte de la ville** lä pôrt də lä vēl

city hall	**l'hôtel** *m* **de ville** lōtel də vēl
– walls	**les remparts** *m/pl* lā räNpär
classicism	**le classicisme** lə kläsēsēsm
cloister	**le cloître** lə klô·ät'rə
closed	**fermé** fermā
coat-of-arms	**les armes** *f/pl* läzärm
collection	**la collection** lä kôleksyôN
column	**la colonne** lä kôlôn
convent	**le couvent** lə kōōväN
copy	**la copie** lä kôpē
court, courtyard	**la cour** lä kōōr
cross	**la croix** lä krô·ä
crypt	**la crypte** lä krēpt
discoverer	**le découvreur** lə dākōōvrär
dolmen	**le dolmen** lə dôlmen
dome	**la coupole** lä kōōpôl
drawing	**le dessin** lə deseN
dune	**la dune** lä dēn
dynasty	**la dynastie** lä dēnästē
emperor	**l'empereur** *m* läNprär
empress	**l'impératrice** *f* leNpärätrēs
engraving	**la gravure** lä grävēr
era	**l'époque** *f* lāpôk
excavations	**les fouilles** *f/pl* lā fōō'ē
excursion	**l'excursion** *f* lekskērsyôN
– boat	**la vedette d'excursion** lä vədet deskskērsyôN
exhibition	**l'exposition** *f* lekspōzēsyôN

expressionism	**l'expressionnisme** *m* lekspresyônēsm
façade	**la façade** lä fäsäd
flea market	**le marché aux puces** lə märshā ō pēs
forest	**la forêt** lä fôre
– fire	**l'incendie** *m* **de forêt** leNsäNdē də fôre
fort	**le fort** lə fôr
fortress	**le château fort** lə shätō fôr
fountain	**la fontaine** lä fôNten
fresco	**la fresque** lä fresk
frieze	**la frise** lä frēz
gable	**le pignon** lə pēnyôN
Gallo-Roman	**gallo-romain** gälō-rômeN
garden	**le jardin** lə zhärdeN
gate	**la porte** lä pôrt
glass	**le verre** lə ver
Gothic	**gothique** gôtēk
hall	**la salle** lä säl
harbor	**le port** lə pôr
historical part of the city/town	**la vieille ville** lä vyey vēl
history	**l'histoire** *f* lēstô·är
house	**la maison** lä mezôN
Impressionism	**l'impressionnisme** *m* leNpresyônēsm
influence	**l'influence** *f* leNflē·äNs
inscription	**l'inscription** *f* leNskrēpsyôN
inventor	**l'inventeur** *m* leNväNtār

Jewish	**juif** zhē-ēf	
king	**le roi** lə rô-ä	
lake	**le lac** lə läk	
landscape	**le paysage** lə pā-ēzäzh	
list of hotels	**la liste des hôtels** lä lēst däzôtel	
main entrance	**le portail** lə pôrtä'ē	
to make a video	**filmer** fēlmā	
map	**le plan** lə pläN	
marble	**le marbre** lə märb'rə	
market	**le marché** lə märshā	
covered –	**les halles** *f/pl* lā äl	
mausoleum	**le mausolée** lə mōsôlā	
memorial	**le site commémoratif** lə sēt kômāmôrätēf	
Middle Ages	**le Moyen-Âge** lə mô-äyenäzh	
mill	**le moulin** lə mōōleN	
minaret	**le minaret** lə mēnäre	
model	**la maquette** lä mäket	
modern	**moderne** môdern	
monastery	**le monastère** lə mônäster	
monument	**le monument** lə mônēmäN	
mosaic	**la mosaïque** lä môzä-ēk	
mosque	**la mosquée** lä môskā	
mountains	**les montagnes** *f/pl* lā môNtän'yə	
museum	**le musée** lə mēzā	
Muslim	**le musulman** lə mēzēlmäN	
narrated slide show	**le spectacle Son et Lumière** lə spektäk'lə sôN ā lēmyer	
national park	**le parc national** lə pärk näsyônäl	

5

nature park	**la réserve zoologique**
	lä räzerv zō·ôlôzhēk
nature preserve	**le site naturel protégé**
	lə sēt nätērel prôtäzhā
nave	**la nef** lä nef
Neoclassicism	**le néoclassicisme**
	lə nā·ôkläsēsēsm
open	**ouvert** ōōver
opera	**l'opéra** *m* lôpärä
original	**l'original** *m* lôrēzhēnäl
ornamentation	**les ornements** *m/pl* lāzôrnəmäN
painter	**le peintre** lə peNt′rə
painting	**la peinture** lä peNtēr
palace	**le palais** lə päle
panorama	**le panorama** lə pänôrämä
park	**le parc** lə pärk
pass	**le col** lə kôl
pedestrian zone	**la zone piétonne** lä zōn pyätôn
photograph	**la photo** lä fōtō
to photograph	**prendre des photos**
	präNd′rə dā fōtō
picture	**le tableau** lə täblō
pilgrim	**le pèlerin** lə pelreN
pilgrimage	**le pèlerinage** lə pelrēnäzh
pillar	**le pilier** lə pēlyä
portal	**le portail** lə pôrtä′ē
portrait	**le portrait** lə pôrtre
poster	**l'affiche** *f* läfēsh
pottery	**la poterie** lä pôtrē

Protestant	**protestant** prôtestäN
queen	**la reine** lä ren
to reconstruct	**reconstituer** rəkôNstētē̄·ā
region	**la région** lä räzhē·ôN
relief	**le relief** lə rəlyef
religion	**la religion** lä rəlēzhyôN
remains	**les vestiges** *m/pl* lā vestēzh
Renaissance	**la Renaissance** lä rənesäNs
reservoir	**le lac de barrage** lə läk də bäräzh
to restore	**restaurer** restôrā
river	**la rivière** lä rēvyer
Roman	**romain** rômeN
Romanesque	**l'art** *m* **roman** lär rômäN
Romans	**les Romains** *m/pl* lā rômeN
Romanticism	**le romantisme** lə rômäNtēsm
roof	**le toit** lə tô·ä
ruins	**les ruines** *f/pl* lā rē̄·ēn
sand	**le sable** lə säb'lə
-stone	**le grès** lə gre
sculptor	**le sculpteur** lə skēlptạr
sculpture	**la sculpture** lä skēlptēr
sights	**les curiosités** *f/pl* lā kēryōzētā
slide	**la diapositive** lä dyäpōzētēv
square *(in town)*	**la place** lä pläs
stadium	**le stade** lə städ
stalactite cave	**la grotte à concrétions** lä grôt ä kôNkrāsyôN
statue	**la statue** lä stätē̄
still life	**la nature morte** lä nätēr môrt

5

street map	**le plan de la ville**	lə pläN də lä vēl
stucco	**le stuc**	lə stēk
style	**le style**	lə stēl
surrounding area	**les environs** *m/pl*	lāzäNvērôN
synagogue	**la synagogue**	lä sēnägôg
tapestry	**la tapisserie**	lä täpēsrē
temple	**le temple**	lə täNp'lə
theater	**le théâtre**	lə tā·ät'rə
tomb	**la tombe**	lä tôNb
tour	**la visite**	lä vēzēt
tourist guide	**le guide**	lə gēd
tourist-information office	**l'office** *m* **du tourisme**	lôfēs dē tōōrēsm
tower	**la tour**	lä tōōr
treasure chamber	**le trésor**	lə trāzôr
valley	**la vallée**	lä välā
vase	**le vase**	lə väz
vault	**la voûte**	lä vōōt
view	**la vue**	lä vē
vineyards	**les vignobles** *m/pl*	lä vēnyôb'lə
to visit	**visiter**	vēzētā
volcano	**le volcan**	lə vôlkäN
wall	**le mur**	lə mēr
waterfall	**la cascade**	lä käskäd
window	**la fenêtre**	lä fənet'rə
wine cellar	**le caveau à vin**	lə kävō ä veN
wine tasting	**la dégustation de vin**	lä dāgēstäsyôN də veN

wine-makers' guild	**la coopérative vinicole**
	lä kô-ôpärätēv vēnēkôl
winery	**la propriété vinicole**
	lä prôprē-ätā vēnēkôl
wing	**l'aile** *f* lel
wooden engraving	**la gravure sur bois** lä grävēr sēr bô-ä
work	**l'œuvre** *f* lãv'rə
zoo	**le zoo** lə zô-ô

INFO There are many wildlife parks in France, some with exotic animals and some with animals in danger of extinction (e.g., eagles, wolves). One of the most famous is the **Réserve de loups des Cévennes**. In the Camargue, an 800 km² (app. 288 square miles) nature reserve in southern France, you will encounter a unique world of plants and animals. The Camargue is famous for its wild white horses, flamingos, and black bulls. In the Pyrenees there are still some bears living in the wild. And on the Côte d'Azur some cities – Antibes, for example – have dolphin aquariums.

5

Animals

bear	**l'ours** m lōōrs
bull	**le taureau** lə tôrō
dolphin	**le dauphin** lə dôfeN
eagle	**l'aigle** m leg'lə
horse	**le cheval** lə shəväl
lizard	**le lézard** lə lāzär
seagull	**la mouette** lä mōō-et
stork	**la cigogne** lä sēgôn'yə

Plants

broom	**le genêt** lə gene
century plant	**l'agave** m lägäv
cork oak	**le chêne-liège** lə shen-lyezh
cypress	**le cyprès** lə sēpre
eucalyptus tree	**l'eucalyptus** m läkälēptēs
fig tree	**le figuier** lə fēgyā
heather	**la bruyère** lä brēyer
holm (oak) tree	**le chêne vert** lə shen ver
lavender	**la lavande** lä läväNd
Mediterranean brushwood	**le maquis** lə mäkē
oak tree	**le chêne** lə shen
oleander	**le laurier-rose** lə lôryā-rōz
olive tree	**l'olivier** m lôlēvyā
orange tree	**l'oranger** m lôräNzhā
palm tree	**le palmier** lə pälmyā
pine tree	**le pin (maritime)** lə peN (märētēm)

132

Shopping

BASIC PHRASES

Where can I get ...? **Où est-ce que je peux acheter ...?**
ōō eskə zhə pā ȧshtā ...?

? Vous désirez? vōō dāzērā? May I help you?

? Est-ce que je peux vous aider? Can I help you with
eskə zhə pā vōōzȧdā? something?

Thanks, but I'm just **Merci, je regarde seulement.**
looking. mersē, zhə rəgȧrd sālmäN.

Someone's already **Merci, on me sert.** mersē, ôN mə ser.
helping me, thanks.

I'd like ... **Je voudrais ...** zhə vōōdre ...

May I have ..., please? **Donnez-moi ..., s'il vous plaît.**
dônā-mô·ä ..., sēl vōō ple.

a can of ... **une boîte de ...** ēn bô·ȧt də ...
a bottle of ... **une bouteille de ...** ēn bōōte'ē də ...
a jar of ... **un pot de ...** eN pô də ...
a pack of ... **un paquet de ...** eN päke də ...

! Je regrette, nous n'avons plus I'm sorry, but we
de ... zhə rəgret, nōō nävôN plē don't have any
də ... more ...

How much *is/are* ...? **Combien *coûte/coûtent* ...?**
kôNbyeN *kōōt/kōōt* ...?

| I don't really like that. | **Cela ne me plaît pas tellement.** |
| | sələ nə mə ple pä telmäN. |

| Could you show me something else? | **Vous pourriez me montrer autre chose?** vōō pōōryā mə môNtrā ōt'rə shōz? |

| Do you have anything less expensive? | **Vous n'auriez rien de moins cher?** vōō nôryā ryeN də mô·N sher? |

INFO Stores in France are generally open until 7 or 7:30 p.m.; smaller grocery stores may be open a bit longer. They are frequently closed at lunchtime from 12 p.m. to 2 p.m. Grocery stores, bakeries, and butchers might also be open on Sunday mornings, but most stores are closed on Monday mornings.

| I'll have to think about it. | **Je dois encore réfléchir.** zhə dô·ä äNkôr rāflāshēr. |

| I like this. I'll take it. | **Cela me plaît. Je le prends.** sələ mə ple. zhə lə präN. |

| **?** | **Vous désirez encore quelque chose?** vōō dāzērā äNkôr kelkə shōz? | Will there be anything else? |

| That's all, thank you. | **Merci, ce sera tout.** mersē, sə sərä tōō. |

| Can I pay with this credit card? | **Est-ce que je peux payer avec cette carte de crédit?** eskə zhə pä pāyā ävek set kärt də krädē? |

May I have a bag for it?	**Vous auriez un sac en plastique?** vōōzôryā eN säk äN plästēk?
Could you wrap it, please?	**Vous pourriez me l'emballer?** vōō pōōryā mə läNbälä?
How much does that cost?	**Ça coûte combien?** sä kōōt kôNbyēN?
Would you give me a receipt, please?	**Vous pourriez me donner un reçu, s'il vous plaît?** vōō pōōryā mə dônä eN rəsē, sēl vōō ple?
This is broken. Do you think you could fix it?	**C'est cassé. Vous pouvez le réparer?** se käsä. vōō pōōvä lə räpärä?
When will it be ready?	**Ce sera prêt quand?** sə sərä pre käN?
I'd like to *exchange*/ *return* this.	**Je voudrais *échanger*/*rendre* cela.** zhə vōōdre *äshäNzhā*/*räNd'*rə sälä.
I'd like a refund, please.	**Je voudrais être remboursé.** zhə vōōdre et'rə räNbōōrsä.
Excuse me, but you haven't given me enough change. I'm short ...	**Vous ne m'avez pas assez rendu. Il manque ...** vōō nə mävä päzäsä räNdē. ēl mäNk ...

136

bag	**le sac** lə säk
better	**meilleur** meyār
big	**grand** gräN
bigger	**plus grand** plē gräN
bottle	**la bouteille** lä bōōte'ē
to buy	**acheter** äshtā
can	**la boîte** lä bô·ät
to cost	**coûter** kōōtā
check	**le chèque** lə shek
classic	**classique** kläsēk
credit card	**la carte de crédit** lä kärt də krädē
to exchange	**échanger** äshäNzhā
expensive	**cher** sher
to give	**donner** dônā
present	**le cadeau** lə kädō
heavy	**lourd** lōōr
jar	**le pot** lə pô
less expensive	**moins cher** mô·eN sher
light *(weight)*	**léger** lāzhā
modern	**moderne** môdern
money	**l'argent** *m* lärzhäN
more expensive	**plus cher** plē sher
narrow	**étroit** ātrô·ä
package	**le paquet** lə päke
receipt	**le reçu** lə rəsē
to return	**rendre** räNd(rə)
round	**rond** rôN
sale(s)	**les soldes** *f/pl* lä sôld

self-service	**le libre-service** lə lēb'rə-servēs
to sell	**vendre** väNd'rə
to serve	**servir** servēr
shop window	**la vitrine** lä vētrēn
to show	**montrer** môNtrā
small	**petit** pətē
smaller	**plus petit** plē pətē
soft	**mou** mōō
special offer	**l'article** *m* **en promotion** lärtēk'lə äN prômôsyôN
to take	**prendre** präNd'rə
thick	**épais** āpe
thin	**mince** meNs
too ...	**trop ...** trō ...
wide	**large** lärzh

INFO You can purchase only meat in the **boucherie**; sausages and ham are offered in the **charcuterie**. These stores are quite commonly combined into a **boucherie-charcuterie**, where you can get both. You can get prepared foods and appetizers in the **rôtisserie** and from the **traiteur**. Milk products are sold in the **crémerie**: **lait** (milk), **yaourt** (yogurt), **fromage blanc** (cream cheese), and a great many different kinds of cheese. In the **boulangerie** you can buy bread and baked goods as well as simple cakes. If you wish to purchase more elaborate cakes and tarts, visit the **pâtisserie**. By the way, the **magasin libre-service** is a self-service store, frequently a small supermarket.

Colors and Patterns

beige	**beige** bezh
black	**noir** nô·är
blue	**bleu** blā
brown	**marron** *(inv)* märôN
colorful	**multicolore** mēltēkôlôr
dark	**... foncé** ... fôNsā
gold(en)	**doré** dôrā
gray	**gris** grē
green	**vert** ver
light *(color)*	**... clair** ... kler
patterned	**imprimé** eNprēmā
pink	**rose** rōz
purple	**violet** vyôle
red	**rouge** rōōzh
silver	**argent** *(inv)* ärzhäN
solid *(of color)*	**uni** ēnē
striped	**rayé** rāyā
white	**blanc** bläN
yellow	**jaune** zhōn

INFO If you have rented a vacation home or are camping and will be catering for yourself, you will probably go shopping at the **supermarchés** (supermarkets) or **hypermarchés** (superstores). They are usually located on the outskirts of town so that you will probably need a car to get to them. You can get everything there. Tip: tank up your car there, too; gas is usually cheaper there than at a normal gas station.

antique shop	**le magasin d'antiquités, le brocanteur** lə mägäzeN däNtēkētā, lə brókäNtār
baker	**la boulangerie** lä bōōläNzhrē
barber	**le coiffeur** lə kô·äfär
beauty shop	**salon de beauté** sälôN də bōtā
bookstore	**la librairie** lä lēbrerē
butcher's shop	**la boucherie** lä bōōshrē
camera store	**le magasin d'articles photographiques** lə mägäzeN därtēk'lə fōtōgräfēk
candy store	**la confiserie** lä kôNfēzrē
confectionery	**la pâtisserie** lä pätēsrē
dairy (store)	**la crémerie** lä kremrē
delicatessen	**l'épicerie** *f* **fine** lāpēsrē fēn
delicatessen *(cold cuts etc.)*	**la charcuterie** lä shärkētrē
department store	**le grand magasin** lə gräN mägäzeN
dry cleaner's	**le pressing** lə presēng
drugstore	**la droguerie** lä drógrē
electrician's	**le magasin d'électroménager** lə mägäzeN dälektrōmānäzhā
fish store	**la poissonnerie** lä pô·äsônrē
flower shop	**le fleuriste** lə flärēst
grocery store	**l'épicerie** *f* lāpēsrē
hair dresser's	**le coiffeur** lə kô·äfār
jewelry store	**le bijoutier** lə bēzhōōtyā
laundromat	**la laverie automatique** lä lävrē ôtômätēk
leather-goods store	**la maroquinerie** lä märókēnrē

music store	**le magasin de disques**
	lə mägäzeN də dēsk
newsstand	**le marchand de journaux, le kiosque**
	lə märshäN də zhōōrnō, lə kē·ôsk
optician's	**l'opticien** *m* lôptēsyeN
perfume store	**la parfumerie** lä pärfēmrē
shoe store	**le magasin de chaussures**
	lə mägäzeN də shôsēr
shoe-repair shop	**le cordonnier** lə kôrdônyā
shopping center	**le centre commercial**
	lə säNt'rə kômersyäl
souvenir store	**le magasin de souvenirs**
	lə mägäzeN də sōōvnēr
sporting-goods store	**le magasin d'articles de sport**
	lə mägäzeN därtēk'lə də spôr
supermarket	**le supermarché** lə sēpermärshā
tobacconist	**le bureau de tabac** lə bērō də täbä

INFO Particularly in the summer you might often see the sign **Brocante**, indicating one of the numerous second-hand markets or shops, where it might well be worthwhile to have a look around. The **magasin d'antiquités**, on the other hand, sells valuable antiques.

FOOD

What's that? | **Qu'est-ce que c'est?** keskə se?

Could I have ..., please? | **Donnez-moi ..., s'il vous plaît.**
dônā-mô·à ..., sēl vōō ple.

100 grams of ... | **cent grammes de ...** säN gräm də ...
a quarter of ... | **un quart de ...** eN kär də ...
(half) a pound of ... | **une (demi-)livre de ...**
ēn (dəmē-)lēv'rə də ...
a kilo of ... | **un kilo de ...** eN kēlō də ...
a slice of ... | **une tranche de ...** ēn träNsh də ...
a piece of ... | **un morceau de ...** eN môrsō də ...
(half) a liter of ... | **un (demi-)litre de ...**
eN (dəmē-)lēt'rə də ...

A little *less/more*, please. | **Un peu *moins/plus*, s'il vous plaît.**
eN pə̄ mô·N/plēs, sēl vōō ple.

May I try some (of that)? | **Je peux goûter (de ça)?** zhə pə̄ gōōtā
(də sä)?

Food

alcohol-free beer	**la bière sans alcool** lä byer säN älkôl
apple	**la pomme** lä pôm
– juice	**le jus de pomme** lə zhē də pôm
apricot	**l'abricot** *m* äbrēkō
artichoke	**l'artichaut** *m* lärtēshō
artificial sweetener	**la saccharine** lä säkärēn

avocado	**l'avocat** *m*	lävôkä
baby food	**les aliments** *m/pl* **pour bébés**	
		läzälēmäN pōōr bābä
banana	**la banane**	lä bänän
basil	**le basilic**	lə bäzēlēk
beans	**les haricots** *m/pl*	lä ärēkō
beef	**le bœuf**	lə bəf
beer	**la bière**	lä byer
Belgian endive	**l'endive** *f*	läNdēv
bread	**le pain**	lə peN
white –	**le pain blanc**	lə peN bläN
broccoli	**le brocoli**	lə brôkôlē
butter	**le beurre**	lə bər
cake	**le gâteau**	lə gätō
candy	**les chocolats** *m/pl*	lä shôkôlä
canned goods	**les conserves** *f/pl*	lä kôNserv
carrot	**la carotte**	lä kärôt
celery	**le céleri**	lə sälrē
cheese	**le fromage**	lə frômäzh
cherries	**les cerises** *f/pl*	lä sərēz
chestnuts	**les marrons** *m/pl*	lä märôN
chicken	**le poulet**	lə pōōle
chocolate	**le chocolat**	lə shôkôlä
chop *(meat)*	**la côtelette**	lä kôtlet
cider	**le cidre**	lə sēd'rə
cocoa	**le cacao**	lə käkä·ō
coffee	**le café**	lə käfä
cold cuts	**la charcuterie**	lä shärkē̜trē
condensed milk	**le lait condensé**	lə le kôNdäNsä

cookies	**les biscuits** *m/pl* lā bēskē·ē
corn	**le maïs** lə mà-ēs
cream	**la crème** lä krem
cucumber	**le concombre** lə kôNkôNb'rə
cutlet	**l'escalope** *f* leskälôp
dates	**les dattes** *f/pl* lā dät
egg	**l'œuf** *m, pl:* **les œufs** lᴀf, *pl:* lāzᴀ
eggplant	**l'aubergine** *f* lōberzhēn
figs	**les figues** *f/pl* lā fēg
fish	**le poisson** lə pô·äsôN
fruit	**les fruits** *m/pl* lā frē·ē
garlic	**l'ail** *m* lä'ē
grapes	**les raisins** *m/pl* lā rezeN
ground meat	**la viande hachée** lä vyäNd äshā
ham	**le jambon** lə zhäNbôN
boiled –	**le jambon cuit** lə zhäNbôN kē·ē
smoked –	**le jambon cru** lə zhäNbôN krē
herbal tea	**l'infusion** *f* leNfēzyôN
herbs	**les fines herbes** *f/pl* lā fēnəzerb
honey	**le miel** lə myel
jam	**la confiture** lä kôNfētēr
juice	**le jus** lə zhē
ketchup	**le ketchup** lə ketshäp
lamb	**l'agneau** *m* länyō
lemon	**le citron** lə sētrôN
lettuce	**la laitue** lä letē
liver pâté	**le pâté de foie** lə pätā də fô·ä

margarine	**la margarine** lä märgärēn
mayonnaise	**la mayonnaise** lä mäyônez
meat	**la viande** lä vyäNd
melon	**le melon** lə melôN
milk	**le lait** lə le
skim –	**le lait demi-écrémé** lə le dəmē-äkrämä
whole –	**le lait entier** lə le äNtyā
mineral water	**l'eau** *f* **minérale** lō mēnäräl
oatmeal	**les flocons** *m/pl* **d'avoine** lā flôkôN dävô·än
oil	**l'huile** *f* lē·ēl
olive –	**l'huile** *f* **d'olive** lē·ēl dôlēv
olives	**les olives** *f/pl* läzôlēv
onion	**l'oignon** *m* lônyôN
orange	**l'orange** *f* lôräNzh
– juice	**le jus d'orange** lə zhē dôräNzh
parsley	**le persil** lə persē
pasta	**les pâtes** *f/pl* lā pät
peach	**la pêche** lä pesh
pear	**la poire** lä pô·är
pepper *(spice)*	**le poivre** lə pô·äv'rə
pepper *(vegetable)*	**le poivron** lə pô·ävrôN
pickle	**le cornichon** lə kôrnēshôN
pistacchios	**les pistaches** *f/pl* lā pēstäsh
pork	**le cochon, le porc** lə kôshôN, lə pôr
potatoes	**les pommes** *f/pl* **de terre** lā pôm də ter
poultry	**la volaille** lä vôlä'ē

pumpernickel	**le pain noir** lə peN nô·är
rice	**le riz** lə rē
rolls	**les petits pains** *m/pl* lā pətē peN
salt	**le sel** lə sel
sausage *(smoked)*	**le saucisson** lə sôsēsôN
sausage *(raw)*	**la saucisse** lä sôsēs
soft drink	**la limonade** lä lēmônäd
spices	**les épices** *f/pl* lāzpēs
spinach	**les épinards** *m/pl* lāzāpēnär
steak	**le steak** lə stek
strawberries	**les fraises** *f/pl* lā frez
sugar	**le sucre** lə sēk'rə
– cubes	**le sucre en morceaux** lə sēkräN môrsō
tea	**le thé** lə tā
– bag	**le sachet de thé** lə säshe də tā
tomato	**la tomate** lä tômät
tuna	**le thon** lə tôN
veal	**le veau** lə vô
vegetables	**les légumes** *m/pl* lā lāgēm
vinegar	**le vinaigre** lə vēneg'rə
walnuts	**les noix** *f/pl* lā nô·ä
watermelon	**la pastèque** lä pästek
wine	**le vin** lə veN
red –	**le vin rouge** lə veN rōōzh
white –	**le vin blanc** lə veN bläN
yogurt	**le yaourt** lə ē·ä·ōōr
zucchini	**les courgettes** *f/pl* lā kōōrzhet
zwieback	**les biscottes** *f/pl* lā bēskôt

INFO Next to cheese and wine, people also associate France with the **baguette**: this long, crusty loaf of white bread is never missing from the table at any meal. There are also many other kinds of bread made from the same dough in every size and shape imaginable: for example the long, thin version of the baguette, called a **flûte** or **ficelle**, or the broad, large **pain**. Recently the French have been expanding their repertoire of bread, making for example **pain complet** (whole-wheat bread), **pain de campagne** (rustic bread), or **pain de seigle** (rye bread). You can even find the traditional white pan loaf (**pain de mie**) and crisp bread (**pain croustillant**) almost everywhere.

The **marché** (farmer's market) is held once a week; particularly if you are in southern France, you should try to visit it. The large selection of fruit and vegetables creates a colorful feast for the eyes, and you can purchase many regional specialities at good prices. The **Halles** (Parisian market halls) no longer exist, but many parts of Paris and other cities still maintain their tradition. Their covered markets are open every day, even Sunday mornings. The atmosphere in these markets is unique, well worth a visit.

SOUVENIRS

What products are typical of this area?	**Quels sont les produits régionaux typiques?** kel sôN lā prôdē̄-ē rāzhē̄-ônō tēpēk?
Is this handmade?	**Est-ce que c'est fait à la main?** eskə se fe ä lä meN?
Is this *antique/ genuine*?	**Est-ce que c'est *ancien/du vrai*?** eskə se äNsyeN/dē̄ vre?

Souvenirs

belt	**la ceinture** lä seNtēr
blanket	**la couverture** lä kōōvertēr
bowl *(for drinking)*	**le bol** lə bôl
crafts	**l'artisanat** *m* lärtēzänä
dishes	**la vaisselle** lä vesel
fines herbes	**les herbes** *f/pl* **de Provence** läzerb də prôväNs
goblet	**le gobelet** lə gôble
handbag	**le sac à main** lə säk ä meN
handcrafted	**artisanal** ärtēzänäl
handcrafted item	**le produit artisanal** lə prôdē̄-ē ärtēzänäl
handmade	**fait à la main** fetä lä meN
jewelry	**les bijoux** *m/pl* lā bēzhōō
lace	**la dentelle** lä däNtel
lavender	**la lavande** lä läväNd
leather	**le cuir** lə kē̄-ēr
pottery	**la poterie** lä pôtrē̄

148

ceramics	**la céramique** lä sārämēk
shoulder bag	**le sac à bandoulière**
	lə säk ä bäNdōōlyer
silk scarf	**le foulard de soie** lə fōōlär də sô·ä
souvenir	**le souvenir** lə sōōvnēr
stoneware	**la faïence** lä fäyäNs
tablecloth	**la nappe** lä näp
embroidered –	**la nappe brodée** lä näp brôdā
typical	**typique** tēpēk
vase	**le vase** lə väz

CLOTHES AND DRY CLEANER'S

I'm looking for ... **Je cherche ...** zhə shersh ...

? **Quelle est votre taille?** What size are you?
kel e vôt'rə tä'ē?

I'm a European size ... **Je porte du ...** zhə pôrt dē ...

Do you have this in **Est-ce que vous l'avez dans une autre**
another *size/color*? *taille/couleur?* eskə vōō lävā däNzēn
ôt'rə *tä·ē/kōōlar*?

➡ *Colors and Patterns (p. 139)*

May I try this on? **Je peux l'essayer?** zhə pā lāsāyā?

Do you have a mirror? **Vous avez une glace?** vōōzävä ēn gläs?

What kind of material **C'est en quel tissu?** setäN kel tisē?
is this made of?

| It doesn't fit. | **Cela ne me va pas.** |
| | sälä nə mə vä pä. |

| It's too *big/small.* | **C'est trop *grand/petit.*** |
| | se trō gräN/pətē. |

➡ *Basic Phrases (p. 134)*

| This fits perfectly. | **Cela va parfaitement.** |
| | sälä vä pärfetmäN. |

| I'd like to get this dry-cleaned. | **Je voudrais faire nettoyer cela.** |
| | zhə vōōdre fer netō·äyā sälä. |

| Can you get rid of this stain? | **Vous pouvez enlever cette tache?** |
| | vōō pōōvā äNləvā set täsh? |

Clothes and Dry Cleaner's

belt	**la ceinture** lä seNtēr
blouse	**le chemisier** lə shemēzyā
bra	**le soutien-gorge** lə sōōtyeN-gôrzh
cap	**le bonnet** lə bône
coat	**le manteau** lə mäNtō
collar	**le col** lə kôl
color	**la couleur** lä kōōlār
cotton	**le coton** lə kôtôN
denim	**le jean** lə dzhēn
dress	**la robe** lä rôb
to dry-clean	**nettoyer (à sec)**
	netō·äyā (ä sek)
elegant	**élégant** älägäN
to fit	**aller** älā

150

jacket	**la veste** lä vest	
leather	**le cuir** lə kē̇-ēr	
linen	**le lin** lə leN	**6**
long	**long** lôN	
material	**la matière** lä mätyer	
nightgown	**la chemise de nuit**	
	lä shəmēz də nē̇·e	
pants	**le pantalon** lə päNtälôN	
pantyhose	**le collant** lə kôläN	
scarf *(knitted)*	**l'écharpe** *f* lāshärp	
scarf *(silk, silky)*	**le foulard** lə fōōlär	
shirt	**la chemise** lä shəmēz	
short	**court** kōōr	
shorts	**le short** lə shôrt	
silk	**la soie** lä sô·ä	
size *(clothes)*	**la taille** lä tä'ē	
size *(shoes)*	**la pointure** lä pô·eNtēr	
skirt	**la jupe** lä zhēp	
sleeves	**les manches** *f/pl* lā mäNsh	
long –	**les manches** *f/pl* **longues**	
	lā mäNsh lôNg	
short –	**les manches** *f/pl* **courtes**	
	lā mäNsh kōōrt	
socks	**les chaussettes** *f/pl* lä shôset	
knee –	**les mi-bas** *m/pl* lä mē-bä	
sports coat	**le veston** lə vestôN	
sun hat	**le chapeau de soleil**	
	lə shäpō də sôle'ē	
sweater	**le pullover** lə pēlōver	

sweatsuit	**la tenue de jogging**
	lä tənē də dzhôgēng
T-shirt	**le T-shirt** lə tā-shərt
terry cloth	**le tissu éponge** lə tēsē āpôNzh
tie	**la cravate** lä krävät
to try on	**essayer** esāyā
underpants	**le slip** lə slēp
wool	**la laine** lä len

SHOES

| I'd like a pair of ... | **Je voudrais une paire de ...** |
| | zhə vōōdre ēn per də ... |

? **Quelle est votre pointure?** kel e vôt′rə pô·eNtēr? What size do you take?

| I take size ... | **Ma pointure est ...** mä pô·eNtēr e ... |

The heel is too *high/low* for me. **Le talon est trop *haut/plat*.** lə tälôN e trō ō/plä.

They're too *big/small*. **Elles sont trop *grandes/petites*.** el sôN trō gräNd/pəfēt.

They're too tight around here. **Elles me serrent ici.** el mə ser ēsē.

Would you fix the heels, please?	**(Réparez) les talons, s'il vous plaît.**
	(rāpárā) lā tälôN, sēl vōō ple.
Could you resole the shoes, please?	**Un ressemelage, s'il vous plaît.**
	eN rəsemläzh, sēl vōō ple.

Shoes

boots	**les bottes** *f/pl* lā bôt
heel	**le talon** lə tälôN
hiking boots	**les chaussures** *f/pl* **de randonnée**
	lā shōsēr də räNdônā
leather	**le cuir** lə kē̱·ēr
– sole	**la semelle en cuir**
	lä səmel äN kē̱·ēr
pumps	**les escarpins** *m/pl* läzeskärpeN
rubber boots	**les bottes** *f/pl* **en caoutchouc**
	lā bôt äN kä·ōōtshōō
rubber sole	**la semelle en caoutchouc**
	lä səmel äN kä·ōōtshōō
sandals	**les sandales** *f/pl* lā säNdäl
shoelaces	**les lacets** *m/pl* lā läse
shoes	**les chaussures** *f/pl* lā shôsēr
size	**la pointure** lä pô·eNtēr
sneakers	**les baskets** *m/pl* lā bäsket
thongs	**les sandales** *f/pl* **de bain**
	lā säNdäl də beN

WATCHES AND JEWELRY

My watch is *fast/slow*.	**Ma montre *avance/retarde*.**	
Could you have a look at it?	**Vous pourriez la regarder?** äväNs/rətärd. vōō pōōrye lä rəgärdā?	
I'm looking for a nice *souvenir/present*.	**Je cherche un joli *souvenir/cadeau*.** zhə shersh eN zhôlē *sōōvnēr/kädō*.	

? Dans quel prix? däN kel prē? How much would you like to pay?

What's this made of? **C'est en quoi?** setäN kô·ä?

Watches and Jewelry

battery	**la pile** lä pēl	
bracelet	**le bracelet** lə bräsle	
brass	**le cuivre** lə kē·ēv'rə	
brooch	**la broche** lä brôsh	
carat	**le carat** lə kärä	
clip-on earrings	**les clips** *m/pl* lā klēp	
costume jewelry	**le bijou fantaisie** lə bēzhōō fäNtezē	
earrings	**les boucles** *f/pl* **d'oreille** lä bōōk'lə dôre'ē	
gold	**l'or** *m* lôr	
gold-plated	**doré** dôrā	
necklace	**la chaîne** lä shen	
pearl	**la perle** lä perl	
pendant	**le pendentif** lə päNdäNtēf	
plated	**plaqué** pläkā	

154

ring	**la bague** lä bäg
silver	**l'argent** *m* lärzhäN
silver-plated	**argenté** ärzhäNtā
watch	**la montre** lä môNt'rə
-band	**le bracelet de montre**
	lə bräsle də môNt'rə

PERSONAL HYGIENE AND HOUSEHOLD

INFO The **drogueries** in France sell household goods and cleaning products, but only some personal hygiene articles such as soap or toothpaste. You can purchase cosmetics in the **parfumerie**. But recently more and more **drogueries** have started selling cosmetics.

Personal hygiene

aftershave	**la lotion après rasage**
	lä lôsyôN äpre räzäzh
baby bottle	**le biberon** lə bēbrôN
– nipple	**la tétine** lä tätēn
baby oil	**l'huile** *f* **pour bébés** lē·ēl pōōr bābā
baby powder	**la poudre pour bébés**
	lä pōōd(rə) pōōr bābā
bandage *(adhesive)*	**le pansement adhésif**
	lə päNsmäN ädäzēf
blusher	**le blush** lə bläsh
body lotion	**la lotion corporelle** lä lôsyôN kôrpôrel
brush	**la brosse** lä brôs

cleansing cream	**le lait démaquillant**
	lə le dāmäkēyäN
comb	**le peigne** lə pen'yə
condoms	**les préservatifs** *m/pl* lā präzervätēf
cotton (balls)	**le coton** lə kôtôN
cotton swabs	**les Cotons-Tiges** *m/pl (TM)*
	lā kôtôN-tēzh
dental floss	**le fil dentaire** lə fēl däNter
deodorant	**le déodorant** lə dā-ôdôräN
depilatory cream	**la crème dépilatoire**
	lä krem dāpēlätô-är
detergent	**le détergent** lə dāterzhäN
diapers	**les couches** *f/pl* lā kōōsh
disposable ...	**... à jeter** ... ä zhetā
elastic hairband	**l'élastique** *m* **à cheveux**
	lālästēk ä shevā
eye shadow	**l'ombre** *f* **à paupières**
	lôNbrä pôpyer
fragrance-free	**non parfumé** nôN pärfēmā
hair dryer	**le sèche-cheveux** lə sesh-shevā
hairspray	**la laque à cheveux** lä läk ä shevā
handcream	**la crème de soins pour mains**
	lä krem də sô-eN pōōr meN
handkerchiefs	**les mouchoirs** *m/pl* lā mōōshô-är
lip balm	**le stick à lèvres** lə stēk ä lev'rə
lipstick	**le rouge à lèvres** lə rōōzh ä lev'rə
mascara	**le rimmel** lə rēmel
mirror	**le miroir** lə mērô-är

mosquito repellent	**la protection anti-moustiques** lä prôteksyôN äNtē-mōōstēk
nail file	**la lime à ongles** lä lēm ä ôNg'lə
nail polish	**le vernis à ongles** lə vernē ä ôNg'lə
– remover	**le dissolvant** lə dēsôlväN
nailbrush	**la brosse à ongles** lä brôs ä ôNg'lə
night cream	**la crème de nuit** lä krem də nē·ē
pacifier	**la sucette** lä sēset
perfume	**le parfum** lə pärfeN
powder	**la poudre** lä pōōd'rə
razor	**le rasoir** lə razô·är
– blade	**la lame de rasoir** lä läm də räzô·är
shampoo	**le shampooing** lə shäNpōō·eN
shaving cream	**la crème à raser** lä krem ä räzä
shaving foam	**la mousse à raser** lä mōōs ä räzä
shower gel	**le gel douche** lə zhel dōōsh
skin cream	**la crème de soins** lä kräm də sô·eN
soap	**le savon** lə sävôN
SPF (sun protection factor)	**le facteur de protection solaire** lə fäktǝr də prôteksyôN sôler
suncream	**la crème solaire** lä krem sôler
sunscreen *(oil-based)*	**l'huile** *f* **solaire** lē·ēl sôler
sunscreen *(gel-based)*	**le gel solaire** lə zhel sôler
suntan lotion	**le lait solaire** lə le sôler
tampons	**les tampons** *m/pl* lā täNpôN
tissues	**les lingettes** *f/pl* lā leNzhet

toilet paper	**le papier hygiénique**
	lə päpyä ēzhē·änēk
toothbrush	**la brosse à dents** lä brôs ä däN
toothpaste	**le dentifrice** lə däNtēfrēs
tweezers	**la pince à épiler** lä peNs ä äpēlā
washcloth	**le gant de toilette** lə gäN də tô·älet

Household

adapter	**l'adaptateur** *m* lädäptätǝr
alarm clock	**le réveil** lə rāve'ē
aluminum foil	**l'aluminium** *m* **ménager**
	lälēmēnyôm mānäzhä
barbeque	**le barbecue** lə bärbekyōō
battery	**la pile** lä pēl
bottle opener	**le décapsuleur** lə dākäpsēlǝr
broom	**le balai** lə bäle
bucket	**le seau** lə sō
can opener	**l'ouvre-boîte** *m* lōōv'rə-bô·ät
candle	**la bougie** lä bōōzhē
charcoal	**le charbon de bois**
	lə shärbôN də bô·ä
cleaning material	**le produit de nettoyage**
	lə prôdē·ē də netô·äyäzh
clothes pins	**les pinces** *f/pl* **à linge**
	lā peNs ä leNzh
corkscrew	**le tire-bouchon** lə tēr-bōōshôN
cup	**la tasse** lä täs

detergent	**le détergent** lə däterzhäN
dish-washing –	**le liquide vaisselle**
	lə lēkēd vesel
dish cloth	**le chiffon vaisselle** lə shēfôN vesel
extension cord	**la rallonge** lä rälôNzh
flashlight	**la lampe de poche** lä läNp də pôsh
fork	**la fourchette** lä fōōrshet
gas canister	**la cartouche à gaz** lä kärtōōsh ä gäz
glass	**le verre** lə ver
insect repellent	**le spray anti-insectes**
	lə spre äNtē-eNsekt
knife	**le couteau** lə kōōtō
light bulb	**l'ampoule** *f* läNpōōl
lighter	**le briquet** lə brēkā
matches	**les allumettes** *f/pl* läzälēmet
methylated spirit	**l'alcool** *m* **à brûler** lälkôl ä brēlā
napkin	**la serviette** lä servyet
pan	**la poêle** lä pô-äl
paper cup	**le gobelet en carton**
	lə gôble äN kärtôN
paper plate	**l'assiette** *f* **en carton**
	läsyet äN kärtôN
plastic cutlery	**les couverts** *m/pl* **en plastique**
	lä kōōver äN plästēk
plastic wrap	**le film fraîcheur en polyéthylène**
	lə fēlm freshār äN pôlē-ātēlen
plate	**l'assiette** *f* läsyet
pocketknife	**le couteau de poche**
	lə kōōtō də pôsh

pot	**la casserole** lä käsrôl
rag *(for cleaning)*	**la serpillière** lä serpēyer
safety pin	**l'épingle** *f* **de sûreté**
	läpeNg'lǝ dǝ sērtā
scissors	**les ciseaux** *m/pl* lā sēzō
scrubbing brush	**le balai-brosse** lǝ bäle-brôs
sewing needle	**l'aiguille** *f* **à coudre**
	legē'ē ä kōōd'rǝ
sewing thread	**le fil à coudre** lǝ fēl ä kōōd'rǝ
solid fire lighter	**l'allume-feu** *m* lälēm-fā
spoon	**la cuillère** lä kē̱-ēyer
string	**la ficelle** lä fēsel
toothpick	**le cure-dents** lǝ kēr-däN
washing line	**la corde à linge** lä kôrd ä leNzh

AT THE OPTICIAN'S

My glasses are broken.	**Mes lunettes sont cassées.** mā lēnet sôN käsā.
Can you fix this?	**Pouvez-vous réparer cela?** pōōvā-vōō rāpärā sǝlä?
I'm *nearsighted/ farsighted.*	**Je suis** *myope/hypermétrope.* zhǝ svē̱ mē̱-ôp/ēpermātrôp.
I'd like a pair of (prescription) sun-glasses.	**Je voudrais des lunettes de soleil (avec verres correcteurs).** zhǝ vōōdre dā lēnet dǝ sôle'ē (ävek ver kôrektǟr).

| I've *lost/broken* a contact lens. | **J'ai *perdu/cassé* une lentille de contact.** zhā perdē/käsā ēn läNtē'ē də kôNtäkt. |
| I need some *rinsing/cleaning* solution for *hard/soft* contact lenses. | **Il me faudrait une solution de *conservation/nettoyage* pour lentilles *dures/souples*.** ēl mə fôdre ēn sôlēsyôN de kôNservāsyôN/netô·āyäzh pōōr läNtē'ē dēr/sōōp'lə. |

AT THE HAIRDRESSER'S

| I'd like to make an appointment for ... | **Je voudrais un rendez-vous pour ...** zhə vōōdre eN räNdā-vōō pōōr ... |

| **? Qu'est-ce qu'on vous fait?** keskôN vōō fe? | What would you like to have done? |

| Just a trim, please. | **Une coupe seulement.** ēn kōōp sālmäN. |

| I'd like my hair washed, cut, and blow-dried, please. | **Une coupe shampooing-brushing, s'il vous plaît.** ēn kōōp shäNpōō·eN-bräshēng, sēl vōō ple. |

| **? Que désirez-vous comme coupe?** ke dāzērā-vōō kôm kōōp? | How do you want it cut? |

161

I'd like ...	**Je voudrais ...** zhə vōōdre ...
a perm.	**une permanente.** ēn permänäNt.
some highlights put in.	**les mèches.** lā mesh.
to have it colored.	**une coloration.** ēn kôlôräsyôN.

Don't take too much off, please.	**Pas trop court, s'il vous plaît.** pä trō kōōr, sēl vōō ple.

A little more off, please.	**Un peu plus court, s'il vous plaît.** eN pä plē kōōr, sēl vōō ple.

Could you make ... a bit shorter, please?	**Raccourcissez un peu ..., s'il vous plaît.** räkōōrsēsā eN pä ..., sēl vōō ple.
the back	**derrière** deryer
the front	**devant** dəväN
the sides	**de côté** də kôtā
the top	**en haut** äNō

Part it on the *left/right*, please.	**La raie à *gauche/droite*, s'il vous plaît.** lā re ä *gôsh/drô·ät*, sēl vōō ple.

Please trim my beard.	**La barbe, s'il vous plaît.** lā bärb, sēl vōō ple.

Please give me a shave.	**Un rasage, s'il vous plaît.** eN räzäzh, sēl vōō ple.

6

bangs	**la frange** lä fräNzh
beard	**la barbe** lä bärb
black	**noir** nô·är
blond	**blond** blôN
to blow-dry	**faire un brushing** fer eN brāshēng
brown	**brun** breN
to cut	**couper** kōōpā
dandruff	**les pellicules** *f/pl* lā pelēkēl
to dye	**faire une teinture** fer ēn teNtēr
gel	**le gel** lə zhel
gray	**gris** grē
hair	**les cheveux** *m/pl* lā shəvā
– coloring	**la coloration** lä kôlôräsyôN
– spray	**la laque à cheveux** lä läk ä shəvā
dry –	**les cheveux** *m/pl* **secs**
	lā shəvā sek
oily –	**les cheveux** *m/pl* **gras**
	lā shəvā grä
mustache	**la moustache** lä mōōstäsh
perm	**la permanente** lä permänäNt
razor cut	**la coupe au rasoir** lä kōōp ō räzô·är
to shave	**raser** räzā
to wash	**faire un shampooing**
	fer eN shäNpōō·eN

163

PHOTO AND VIDEO

I'd like ...

Je voudrais ... zhə vōōdre ...

a roll of film for this camera.

une pellicule pour cet appareil. ēn pelēkēl pōōr set äpäre'ē.

a *color/black-and-white* film.

une pellicule en *couleurs/noir et blanc*. ēn pelēkēl äN *kōōlär/nō·är ā bläN*.

a slide film.

une pellicule pour diapositives. ēn pelēkēl pōōr dyäpōzētēv.

a film with *24/36* exposures.

une pellicule pour *vingt-quatre/trente-six* photos. ēn pelēkēl pōōr *veNkät'rə/träNtsēs* fōtō.

a VHS video cassette.

une vidéocassette VHS. ēn vēdā·ōkäset vā·äsh·es.

I'd like some batteries for this camera.

Je voudrais des piles pour cet appareil. zhə vōōdre dā pēl pōōr setäpäre'ē.

Could you please put the film in for me?

Vous pouvez me placer la pellicule dans l'appareil? vōō pōōvā mə pläsā lä pelēkēl däN läpäre'ē?

Just develop the negatives, please.

Seulement les négatifs, s'il vous plaît. səlmäN lā nāgätēf, sēl vōō ple.

I'd like a ... × ... picture from each negative, please.

Une épreuve de chaque négatif, format ... sur ..., s'il vous plaît. ēn āprəv də shäk nāgätēf, fôrmä ... sēr ..., sēl vōō ple.

164

When will the pictures be ready?	**Les photos seront prêtes quand?** lā fōtō sərôN pret kāN?
Could you repair my camera?	**Vous pouvez réparer mon appareil photo?** vōō pōōvā rāpārā mônāpāreˈē fōtō?
The film doesn't wind forward.	**Il bloque.** ēl blôk.
The *shutter release/flash* doesn't work.	*Le déclencheur/Le flash* **ne fonctionne pas.** lə dākläNshār/lə fläsh nə fôNksyôn pä.
I'd like to have passport photos taken.	**Je voudrais faire faire des photos d'identité.** zhə vōōdre fer fer dā fōtō dēdäNtētā.
Do you have any ... by ...?	**Avez-vous des ... de ...?** ävā-vōō dā ... də ...?
CD's	**CD** sā-dā
cassettes	**cassettes** käset
records	**disques** dēsk
Do you have ... 's latest cassette?	**Je voudrais la dernière cassette de ...** zhə vōōdre lä dernyer käset də ...
I'm interested in folk music. What would you recommend?	**Je m'intéresse à la musique folklorique. Pourriez-vous me recommander quelque chose?** zhə meNtäres ä lä mēzēk fôlklôrēk. pōōryā-vōō mə rəkômäNdā kelkə shōz?

6

165

automatic shutter release	**le déclencheur automatique** lə däkläNshār ôtômätēk
battery	**la pile** lä pēl
black-and-white film	**la pellicule en noir et blanc** lä pelēkēl äN nô·ä·rā bläN
camcorder	**le caméscope** lə kämäskôp
camera	**l'appareil *m* photo** läpäre'ē fōtō
cassette	**la cassette** lä käset
CDs	**les CD *m/pl*** lā sā-dā
color film	**la pellicule en couleurs** lä pelēkēl äN koolār
color filter	**le filtre coloré** lə fēlt'rə kôlôrā
to expose	**exposer** ekspôzā
film *(camera)*	**la pellicule** lä pelēkēl
film *(movie camera)*	**le film** lə fēlm
to film	**filmer** fēlmā
flash	**le flash** lə fläsh
folk music	**la musique folklorique** lä mēzēk fôlklôrēk
lens	**l'objectif *m*** lôbzhektēv
light meter	**le posemètre** lə pōzmet'rə
light sensitivity	**la sensibilité** lä säNsēbēlētā
music	**la musique** lä mēzēk
negative	**le négatif** lə nägätēf
photo	**la photo** lä fōtō
radio	**la radio** lä rädyō
record	**le disque** lə dēsk
shutter release	**le déclencheur** lə däkläNshār

slide	**la diapo** lä dyäpō	
– film	**la pellicule pour diapositives**	
	lä pelēkēl pōōr dyäpōzētēv	
UV filter	**le filtre UV** lə fēlt're ē-vä	**6**
VHS	**VHS** vä-äsh-es	
video camera	**la caméra vidéo** lä kämärä vēdä-ō	
video cassette	**la vidéocassette** lä vēdä-ōkäset	
video recorder	**le magnétoscope** lə mänyätôskôp	
Walkman®	**le Walkman®** lə ōō-ôkmän	
wide-angle lens	**l'objectif grand angle**	
	lôbzhektēf gräNdäNg'lə	
zoom lens	**le téléobjectif, le zoom**	
	lə tälä-ôbzhektēf, lə zōōm	

READING AND WRITING

I'd like ...	**Je voudrais ...** zhə vōōdre ...
an *American/English* newspaper.	**un journal *américain/anglais*.** eN zhōōrnäl ämärēkeN/äNgle.
an *American/English* magazine.	**un magazine *américain/anglais*.** eN mägäzēn ämärēkeN/äNgle.
a map of the area.	**une carte de la région.** ēn kärt də lä räzhē-ôN.
Do you have a more current issue?	**Vous auriez aussi un journal plus récent?** vōōzôryä ôsē eN zhōōrnäl plē räsäN?

Do you have any books in English?	**Est-ce que vous avez des livres en anglais?** eskə vōōzävä dā lēvränäNgle?
Do you have stamps?	**Est-ce que vous avez aussi des timbres?** eskə vōōzävä ôsē dā teNb'rə?

Reading and Writing

adhesive tape	**le ruban adhésif** lə rēbäN ädäzēf
airmail paper	**le papier à lettres pour courrier aérien** lə päpyä ä let'rə pōōr kōōryä ä·äryeN
ballpoint pen	**le crayon bille** lə kreyôN bē'ē
book	**le livre** lə lēv'rə
colored pencils	**les crayons de couleur** lā kreyôN də kōōlər
coloring book	**le livre à colorier** lə lēv'rə ä kôlôryā
cookbook	**le livre de cuisine** lə lēv'rə də kē̄·ēzēn
dictionary	**le dictionnaire** lə dēksyôner
envelope	**l'enveloppe** *f* läNvəlôp
eraser	**la gomme** lä gôm
glue	**la colle** lä kôl
hiking trail map	**la carte de randonnées pédestres** lä kärt də räNdônä pädest'rə
magazine	**le magazine** lə mägäzēn
map of bicycle routes	**la carte de randonnées cyclistes** lä kärt də rändônä sēklēst
newspaper	**le journal** lə zhōōrnäl
paper	**le papier** lə päpyä

pencil	**le crayon** lə kreyôN
– sharpener	**le taille-crayon** lə tä'ē-kreyôN
picture book	**le livre d'images** lə lēv'rə dēmäzh
playing cards	**les cartes f/pl à jouer** lā kärt ä zhōō-ā
postcard	**la carte postale** lä kärt pôstäl
road map	**la carte routière** lä kärt rōōtyer
stamp	**le timbre** lə teNb'rə
stationery	**le papier á lettres** lə päpyā ä let'rə
street map	**le plan de la ville** lə pläN də lä vēl
travel guide	**le guide de voyage** lə gēd də vô-äyäzh
wrapping paper	**le papier cadeau** lə päpyā kädō
writing pad	**le carnet** lə kärne

AT THE TOBACCONIST'S

A pack of *filtered/
unfiltered* cigarettes,
please.

**Un paquet de cigarettes *avec/sans* filt-
res, s'il vous plaît.** eN päke də sēgäret
ävek/säN fēlt'rə, sēl vōō ple.

A *carton/pack* of ...,
please.

***Une cartouche/Un paquet* de ..., s'il
vous plaît.** ēn kärtōōsh/eN päke də ...,
sēl vōō ple.

A pack of *pipe/ciga-
rette* tobacco, please.

**Un paquet de tabac *pour la pipe/à
cigarettes*, s'il vous plaît.** eN päke də
täbä *pōōr lä pēp/ä sēgäret*, sēl vōō ple.

Could I have *a box of
matches/a lighter*,
please?

***Une boîte d'allumettes/Un briquet*, s'il
vous plaît.** ēn bô-ät däl̠met/eN brēke,
sēl vōō ple.

At the Tobacconist's

box	**la boîte** lä bô·ät
carton	**la cartouche** lä kärtōōsh
cigarettes	**les cigarettes** *f/pl* lā sēgäret
cigarillos	**les cigarillos** *m/pl* lā sēgärēyō
cigars	**les cigares** *m/pl* lā sēgär
lighter	**le briquet** lə brēke
matches	**les allumettes** *f/pl* lāzälēmet
pack	**le paquet** lə päke
pipe	**la pipe** lä pēp
– cleaner	**le cure-pipe** lə kēr-pēp
– tobacco	**le tabac pour la pipe** lə täbä pōōr lä pēp

Entertainment and Sports

SWIMMING AND WATER SPORTS

At the Beach

Is there a beach nearby?	**Est-ce qu'il y a une plage près d'ici?** eskēlyä ēn pläzh pre dēsē?
How do you get to the beach?	**Comment va-t-on à la plage?** kômäN vätôN ä lä pläzh?
Is there any shade there?	**Est-ce qu'il y a de l'ombre là-bas?** eskēlyä də lômb'rə lä-bä?
How *deep/warm* is the water?	**Quelle est la *profondeur/température* de l'eau?** kel e lä *prôfôNdār/tāNpārätār* də lō?

INFO You will see the green flag flying during good weather: it indicates that it is safe to swim within the marked area. If the yellow flag is flying, then only good swimmers should venture into the water. When the red flag is up, bathing is prohibited. In many places in France it is not at all unusual for people to be bathing topless. This is quite normal and not an occasion for you to notify the police. For those who wish to bare all, there are also separate nudist beaches. Dogs are not permitted on French beaches.

Are there strong currents here?	**Est-ce qu'il y a des courants?** eskēlyä dä kōōräN?
Is it dangerous for children?	**C'est dangereux pour les enfants?** se däNzhrā pōōr lāzänfäN?

When is *low/high* tide?	**Quelle est l'heure de la marée *basse/haute*?** kel e lār də lä märä bäs/ōt?
Are there jellyfish around here?	**Est-ce qu'il y a des méduses ici?** eskēlyä dā mādēz ēsē?
Where can I rent ...?	**Où est-ce qu'on peut louer ...?** ōō eskôN pā lōō·ā ...?
I'd like to rent a *lounge chair/beach umbrella.*	**Je voudrais louer *une chaise longue/un parasol*.** zhə vōōdre lōō·ā ēn shez lôNg/eN päräsôl.
I'd like to go water-skiing.	**Je voudrais faire du ski nautique.** zhə vōōdre fer dē skē nōtēk.
I'd like to take *diving/windsurfing* lessons.	**Je voudrais suivre un cours de *plongée/planche à voile*.** zhə vōōdre svēv'rə eN kōōr də plôNzhā/pläNsh ä vô·äl.
I'd like to go deep-sea fishing.	**Je voudrais aller pêcher en haute mer.** zhə vōōdre älā pāshā äN ōt mer.
How much would *an hour/a day* cost?	**Quel est le tarif pour *une heure/une journée*?** kel e lə tärēf pōōr ēnār/ēn zhōōrnä?
Would you keep an eye on my things for a moment, please?	**Vous pourriez surveiller mes affaires un instant, s'il vous plaît?** vōō pōōryā sērvāyā māzäfer eNeNstäN, sēl vōō ple?

7

At the Swimming Pool

How much does it cost to get in?	**Combien coûte l'entrée?** kôNbyeN kōōt läNträ?
What kind of change do I need for the *lockers/hair-dryers*?	**Pour le *vestiaire/sèche-cheveux*, qu'est-ce qu'il me faut comme pièces?** pōōr lə *vestyer/sesh-shəvā̲*, keskēl mə fō kôm pyes?
Is there also a sauna here?	**Est-ce qu'il y a aussi un sauna?** eskēlyä ôsē eN sōnä?
Do I have to wear a bathing cap?	**Je dois porter un bonnet de bain?** zhə dô·ä pôrtā eN bône də beN?
I'd like to rent ...	**Je voudrais louer ...** zhə vōōdre lōō·ä ...
a bathing cap.	**un bonnet de bain.** eN bône də beN.
a towel.	**une serviette.** ē̲n servyet.
some water wings.	**des manchettes gonflables.** dā mäNshet gôNfläb'lə.
Are there swimming courses for children?	**Est-ce qu'il y a des cours de natation pour enfants?** eskēlyä dā kōōr də nätäsyôN pōōr äNfäN?
Where's the *lifeguard/ first-aid station*?	**Où est le *maître-nageur/poste de secours*?** ōō e lə meťrə-näzhā̲r/pôst də səkōōr?

174

air mattress	**le matelas pneumatique** lə mätlä pnǟmätēk
bathing suit	**le maillot (de bain)** lə mäyō (də beN)
bay	**la baie** lä be
beach	**la plage** lä pläzh
– umbrella	**le parasol** lə päräsôl
bikini	**le bikini** lə bēkēnē
boat	**le bateau** lə bätō
– rental	**la location de bateaux** lä lôkäsyôN də bätō
changing room	**la cabine** lä käbēn
current	**le courant** lə kōōräN
to dive	**plonger** plôNzhā
diving board	**le tremplin** lə träNpleN
diving mask	**le masque de plongée** lə mäsk də plôNzhā
diving platform	**le plongeoire** lə plôNzhô·är
fins	**les palmes** *f/pl* lā pälm
heated spa	**le bain thermal** lə beN termäl
inflatable boat	**le bateau pneumatique** lə bätō pnǟmätēk
jellyfish	**la méduse** lä mādēz
lake	**le lac** lə läk
lifeguard	**le maître nageur** lə met'rə-näzhār
lifesaver	**la bouée de sauvetage** lä bōō·ā də sôvtäzh
lounge chair	**la chaise longue** lä shez lôNg
motorboat	**le bateau à moteur** lə bätō ä môtār

175

non-swimmer	**le non-nageur** lə nôN-näzhār	
nudist beach	**la plage naturiste** lä pläzh nätērēst	
pedal boat	**le pédalo** lə pādälō	
rowboat	**le bateau à rames** lə bätō ä räm	
sailboat	**le bateau á voiles** lə bätō ä vô·äl	
to go sailing	**faire de la voile** fer də lä vô·äl	
sand	**le sable** lə säb'lə	
sandy beach	**la plage de sable** lä pläzh də säb'lə	
sauna	**le sauna** lə sōnä	
to go scuba-diving	**plonger** plôNzhā	
scuba gear	**l'équipement** *m* **de plongée** läkēpmäN də plôNzhā	
sea urchin	**l'oursin** *m* lo͞orseN	
shade	**l'ombre** *f* lôNb'rə	
shower	**la douche** lä do͞osh	
snorkel	**le tube de plongée** lə tēb də plôNzhā	
storm	**la tempête** lä täNpet	
sunglasses	**les lunettes** *f/pl* **de soleil** lā lēnet də sôle'ē	
suntan lotion	**la crème solaire** lä krem sôler	
supervised beach	**la plage gardée** lä pläzh gärdā	
surfboard	**la planche à voile** lä pläNsh ä vô·äl	
to go surfing	**faire du surf** fer dē sārf	
swimming trunks	**le caleçon de bain** lə kälsôN də beN	
to go swimming *(as a sport)*	**nager** näzhā	
to go swimming *(for pleasure)*	**se baigner** sə benyā	
swimming pool	**la piscine** lä pēsēn	

176

tide	**la marée** lä märā
high –	**la marée haute** lä märā ōt
low –	**la marée basse** lä märā bäs
towel	**la serviette** lä servyet
water	**l'eau** f lō
– polo	**le ballon de plage** lə bälôN də pläzh
– skiing	**le ski nautique** lə skē nōtēk
– wings	**les manchettes** f/pl **gonflables**
	lā mäNshet gôNfläb'lə
wave	**la vague** lä väg
wet suit	**la combinaison de plongée**
	lä kôNbēnezôN də plôNzhā
to go wind-surfing	**faire de la planche à voile**
	fer də lä pläNsh ä vô·äl

More Sports and Games (p. 183)

MOUNTAINEERING

I'd like to *go to/ climb* ...

Je voudrais *aller à/monter sur le* **...**
zhə vōōdre älä ä/môNtā sȇr lə ...

Can you recommend *an easy/a moderately difficult* trail?

Vous pourriez me recommander une promenade *facile/de difficulté moyenne***?** vōō pōōryā mə rəkômäNdā ēn prômnäd fäsēl/də dēfēkēltā mô·äyen?

About how long will it take?

Combien de temps dure-t-elle environ? kôNbyeN də täN dȇrtel äNvērôN?

177

7

INFO You can find hiking trails, indicated by the abbreviation **GR (Grande Randonée)** and a number, almost anywhere in France. They are well taken care of and always marked with two horizontal white and red stripes. You can spend the night in the **gîtes d'étape** along the way.

Is the trail well marked?	**Le chemin est bien balisé?** lə shəmeN e byeN bälēzā?
Is the trail secure?	**Les passages difficiles sont assurés?** lā päsäzh dēfēsēl sôN äsērā?
Is there anywhere we can get something to eat along the way?	**Est-ce qu'on trouve en route de quoi se restaurer?** eskôN trōōv äN rōōt də kô·ä se restôrā?
Are there guided tours?	**Est-ce qu'il y a des tours guidés?** eskēlyä dā tōōr gēdā?
When does the next cable car go up?	**A quelle heure monte le prochain téléphérique?** ä kelār môNt lə prôsheN tālāfārēk?
When does the last cable car come down?	**A quelle heure descend le dernier téléphérique?** ä kelār dāsäN lə dernyā tālāfārēk?
Is this the right way to ...?	**Est-ce que c'est le bon chemin pour aller à ...?** eskə se lə bôN shəmeN pōōr älā ä ...?
How much further is it to ...?	**C'est encore loin jusqu'à ...?** setäNkôr lô·eN zhēskä ...?

I'm afraid of heights. **Je crains le vertige.** zhə kren lə vertēzh.

Mountaineering

cable car	**le téléphérique** lə tālāfārēk
chair lift	**le télésiège** lə tālāsyezh
to go hiking	**faire des randonnées** fer dā räNdônā
hiking boots	**les chaussures** *f/pl* **de randonnée** lā shôsēr də räNdônā
hiking map	**la carte de randonnée** lä kärt də räNdônā
hiking trail	**le sentier de randonnée** lə säNtyā də räNdônā
hut	**le chalet** lə shäle
mountain	**la montagne** lä môNtän'yə
– climbing	**faire de la montagne** fer də lä môNtän'yə
– climbing boots	**les chaussures de montagne** lā shôsēr də môNtän'yə
– climbing guide	**le guide de montagne** lə gēd də môNtän'yə
ravine	**la gorge** lä gôrzh
rope	**la corde** lä kôrd
shelter	**le refuge** lə rəfēzh
trail	**le chemin, le sentier** lə shəmeN, lə säNtyā

SKIING

I'd like to rent ...   **Je voudrais louer ...** zhə vōōdre lōō·ā ...

   cross-country skis.   **des skis de fond.** dā skē də fôN.

   cross-country
   skiing boots,
   size ...   **des chaussures de ski de fond,
pointure ...** dā shôsēr də skē də fôN,
pô·eNtēr ...

   downhill skis.   **des skis de descente.** dā skē də
desäNt.

   skiing boots,
   size ...   **des chaussures de ski, pointure ...**
dā shôsēr də skē, pô·eNtēr ...

   a snowboard.   **un snowboard.** eN snōbôrd.

   ice skates, size ...   **des patins à glace, pointure ...**
dā pätēN ä gläs, pô·eNtēr ...

   a sled.   **une luge.** ēn lēzh.

I'd like to ...   **Je voudrais ...** zhə vōōdre ...

   enroll my child for
   skiing lessons.   **inscrire mon enfant à l'école de ski.**
eNskrēr mônäNfäNt ä läkôl də skē.

   take a skiing
   course.   **m'inscrire à un cours de ski.**
meNskrēr ä eN kōōr də skē.

   have a private in-
   structor.   **prendre des leçons particulières.**
präNd'rə dā lesôN pärtēkēlyer.

I'm ...   **Je suis ...** zhə svē ...

   a beginner.   **débutant.** dābētäN.

   an average skier.   **un skieur moyen.**
eN skē·ēr mô·äyeN.

   a good skier.   **un bon skieur.** eN bôN skē·ēr.

I'd like a lift pass for ...	**Je voudrais un forfait pour ...** zhə vōōdre eN fôrfe pōōr ...
one/half a day.	***une/une demi-journée.*** *ēn/ēn* dəmē-zhōōrnā.
two days.	**deux jours.** dₐ̈ zhōōr.
a week.	**une semaine.** ēn səmen.

! **Il vous faut une photo d'iden-tité.** ēl vōō fō ēn fōtō dēdäNtētā.

You'll need a pass-port photo.

When is the half-day pass valid?	**Le forfait demi-journée est valable à partir de quelle heure?** lə fôrfe dəmē-zhōōrnā e väläb'lə ä pärtēr də kelₐ̈r?
When do the lifts *start/stop* running?	**Les remontées marchent *à partir de/ jusqu'à* quelle heure?** lā rəmôNtā märsh *ä pärtēr də/zhₑ̈skä* kelₐ̈r?
When is the last downhill run?	**La dernière cabine redescend à quelle heure?** lä dernyer käben rədāsäN ä kelₐ̈r?
Has the cross-country skiing track been set?	**Est-ce que la piste de fond est pré-parée?** eskə lä pēst də fôN e prāpärā?

Skiing

avalanche warning	**le danger d'avalanche**
	lə däNzhā dävälä Nsh
binding	**la fixation** lä fēksäsyôN
children's pass	**le forfait enfants** lə fôrfe äNfäN
cross-country skiing	**le ski de fond** lə skē də fôN
cross-country track	**la piste de ski de fond**
	lä pēst də skē də fôN
downhill run	**la descente** lä dāsäNt
ice-skating	**le patinage sur glace**
	lə pätēnäzh sēr gläs
icy	**verglacé** vergläsā
lift	**la remontée** lä rəmôNtā
piste	**la piste** lä pēst
black –	**la piste noire** lä pēst nô·är
blue –	**la piste bleue** lä pēst blᾱ
red –	**la piste rouge** lä pēst rōōzh
ski instructor	**le moniteur de ski** lə mônētᾱr də skē
ski poles	**les bâtons** *m/pl* **de ski** lā bätôN də skē
ski wax	**le fart** lə färt
skiing	**le ski** lə skē
skiing goggles	**les lunettes** *f/pl* **de ski** lā lēnet də skē
skiing pass	**le forfait de ski** lə fôrfe də skē
snow	**la neige** lä nezh
toboggan course	**la piste de luge** lä pēst də lēzh

MORE SPORTS AND GAMES

Do you have any playing cards/board games?	**Vous avez des cartes à jouer/jeux de société?** vōōzävā dā kärt ä zhōō-ā/zhā də sôsyätā?
What sports do you participate in?	**Quel sport pratiquez-vous?** kel spôr prätēkā-vōō?

INFO Boules or **pétanque** is not simply a sport, with **boules** champions sent to countless **boules** tournaments; **boules** also has an important social function: **boules** players and spectators meet at a specific place, usually in the shade of the tall, leafy plane trees, and the spectators comment on every throw. You can join the game even if you don't speak any French – as long as you know the rules.

I'd like to take a ... course.	**Je voudrais suivre un cours de ...** zhə vōōdre svēv'rə eN kōōr də ...
May I join in?	**Je peux jouer avec vous?** zhə pā zhōō-ā ävek vōō?
We'd like to rent a tennis court for (half) an hour.	**Nous voudrions retenir un court de tennis pour une (demi-)heure.** nōō vōōdrē-ôN rətnēr eN kōōr də tenēs pōōr ēn (dəmē-)är.
I'd like to rent ...	**Je voudrais louer ...** zhə vōōdre lōō-ā ...

aerobics	**l'aérobic** *m* lā-ārôbēk
athletic	**sportif** spôrtēf
badminton	**le badminton** lə bädmēntôn
bait	**l'appât** *m* läpä
ball *(big)*	**le ballon** lə bälôN
ball *(small)*	**la balle** lä bäl
basketball	**le basket** lə bäsket
beginner *(female)*	**la débutante** lä dābētäNt
beginner *(male)*	**le débutant** lə dābētäN
bicycle	**la bicyclette** lä bēsēklet
bike hike	**la randonnée cycliste** lä räNdônā sēklēst
board game	**le jeu de société** lə zhā də sôsyätā
canoe	**le canoë** lə känô-ā
(playing) cards	**les cartes** *f/pl* **à jouer** lā kärt ä zhōō-ā
card game	**le jeu de cartes** lə zhā də kärt
championship	**le championnat** lə shäNpyônä
changing rooms	**les vestiaires** *m/pl* lā vestyer
coach	**l'entraîneur** *m* läNtrenār
coaching session	**l'heure** *f* **d'entraîneur** lār däNtrenār
contest	**la compétition** lä kôNpātēsyôN
course	**le cours** lə kōōr
to cycle	**faire de la bicyclette** fer də lä bēsēklet
doubles *(tennis)*	**le double** lə dōōb'lə
final score	**le score** lə skôr
finishing line	**le but** lə bē
to fish	**pêcher à la ligne** peshā ä lä lēn'yə

184

fishing hook	**l'hameçon** *m* lämsôN
fishing license	**le permis de pêche** lə permē də pesh
fishing rod	**la canne à pêche** lä kän ä pesh
fitness center	**le studio de mise en forme**
	lə stēdyō də mēz äN fôrm
game	**la partie** lä pärtē
gliding	**le deltaplane** lə deltäplän
goal	**le but** lə bē
-keeper	**le gardien de but**
	lə gärdyeN də bē
golf	**le golf** lə gôlf
– club	**le club de golf** lə klēb də gôlf
– course	**le terrain de golf** lə tereN də gôlf
gymnastics	**la gymnastique** lä zhēmnästēk
handball	**le handball** lə äNdbäl
horse	**le cheval** lə shəväl
jazz dancing	**le jazz-dance** lə dzhäz-däNs
to go jogging	**faire du jogging** fer dē dzhôgēng
judo	**le judo** lə zhēdō
kayak	**le kayak** lə käyäk
to lose	**perdre** perd'rə
mini-golf course	**le mini-golf** lə mēnē-gôlf
paragliding	**le parapente** lə päräpäNt
to play	**jouer** zhōō-ā
referee	**l'arbitre** *m* lärbēt'rə
regatta	**la régate** lä rägät
to ride a horse	**faire du cheval** fer dē shəväl
to row	**ramer** rämā
rowboat	**le bâteau à rames** lə bätō ä räm

7

185

sauna	**le sauna** lə sōnä
singles *(tennis)*	**le simple** lə seNp'lə
soccer	**le football** lə fōōtbōl
– game	**le match de football** lə mätsh də fōōtbōl
– field	**le terrain de football** lə tereN də fōōtbōl
solarium	**le solarium** lə sôläryôm
sports	**le sport** lə spôr
– field	**le terrain de sport** lə tereN də spôr
squash	**le squash** lə skväsh
start	**le départ** lə däpär
table tennis	**le ping-pong** lə pēng-pôNg
team	**l'équipe** *f* lākēp
tennis	**le tennis** lə tenēs
– ball	**la balle de tennis** lä bäl də tenēs
– court	**le court de tennis** lä kōōr də tenēs
– racket	**la raquette de tennis** lä räket də tenēs
tie *(of games)*	**match nul** mätsh nēl
victory	**la victoire** lä vēktô·är
volleyball	**le volley** lə vôle
to win	**gagner** gänyā
working out *(exercise)*	**la mise en forme** lä mēz äN fôrm

CULTURE AND FESTIVALS

At the Box Office

à droite ä drô·ät		right
à gauche ä gōsh		left
complet kôNple		sold out
la galerie lä gälrē		gallery
la loge lä lôzh		box
la place lä pläs		seat
la sortie lä sôrtē		exit
la sortie de secours lä sôrtē də səkōōr		emergency exit
le balcon lə bälkôN		balcony
l'entrée *f* läNträ		entrance
le milieu lə mēlyə̄		middle
le parterre lə pärter		orchestra *(seating)*
le rang lə räN		row
l'orchestre *m* lôrkest'ər		orchestra

Do you have a schedule of events?

Est-ce que vous avez un calendrier des manifestations? eskə vōōzävä eN käläNdrē·ä dä mänēfestäsyôN?

INFO French festivals often feature a **corso** (procession) or **corso fleuri** (procession of flowers). On July 14, Bastille Day, there is a **revue** (parade), **feu d'artifice** (fireworks), and a **bal du 14 juillet** (ball for the 14th of July). You might also like to visit a **fête foraine** (carnival). If you are in France during July, you might also come across the **Tour de France**, a cycling race through the entire country.

What's on today?	**Qu'est-ce qu'on donne aujourd'hui?** keskôN dôn ozhōōrdvē?
Where can I get tickets?	**Où est-ce qu'on prend les billets?** ōō eskôN präN lä bēye?
When does the *performance/concert* start?	**A quelle heure commence *la représentation/le concert*?** ä kelär kômäNs *lä rəprāzäNtäsyôN/lə kôNser*?
Can I reserve tickets?	**On peut réserver?** ôN pə rāzervā?
Do you still have tickets for *today/ tomorrow*?	**Vous avez encore des billets pour *aujourd'hui/demain*?** vōōzävā äNkôr dā bēye pōōr *ōzhōōrdvē/dəmeN*?
I'd like *a ticket/two tickets* for ..., please.	**Un billet/Deux billets pour ..., s'il vous plaît.** eN bēye/də bēye pōōr ..., sēl vōō ple.
How much is a ticket?	**Quel est le prix des billets?** kel e lə prē dā bēye?
Is there a discount for ...	**Est-ce qu'il y a des réductions pour ...** eskēlyä dā rādēksyôN pōōr ...
children?	**les enfants?** lāzäNfäN?
senior citizens?	**les personnes du troisième âge?** lā persón də trô-äsyem äzh?
students?	**les étudiants?** lāzätēdyäN?
I'd like to rent an opera glass.	**Je voudrais louer des jumelles.** zhə vōōdre lōō-ā dā zhēmel.

188

act	**l'acte** *m* läkt
actor	**l'acteur** *m* läktãr
actress	**l'actrice** *f* läktrēs
advance booking	**la location** lä lôkäsyôN
ballet	**le ballet** lə bäle
beginning	**le début** lə däbē
box office	**la caisse** lä kes
circus	**le cirque** lə sērk
cloakroom	**le vestiaire** lə vestyer
composer	**le compositeur** lə kôNpôzētãr
concert	**le concert** lə kôNser
conductor	**le chef d'orchestre** lə shef dôrkest'rə
dancer *(male)*	**le danseur** lə däNsãr
dancer *(female)*	**la danseuse** lä däNsãz
director *(film)*	**le réalisateur** lə rä·älēzätãr
director *(female)*	**la réalisatrice** lä rä·älēzätrēs
director *(theater)*	**le metteur en scène** lə metãr äN sen
end	**la fin** lä feN
festival	**le festival** lə festēväl
folklore evening	**la soirée folklorique** lä sô·ärā fôlklôrēk
intermission	**l'entracte** *m* läNträkt
leading role	**le premier rôle** lə prəmyā rōl
movie	**le film** lə fēlm
– theater	**le cinéma** lə sēnämä
music	**la musique** lä mēsēk
musical	**la comédie musicale** lä kômädē mēzēkäl

7

189

opera	**l'opéra** *m* lôpārä
opera singer *(female)*	**la cantatrice** lä käNtätrēs
orchestra	**l'orchestre** *m* lôrkest'rə
original version	**la version originale** lä versyôN ôrēzhēnäl
performance *(movie)*	**la séance** lä sā·äNs
performance *(theater)*	**la représentation** lä rəprāzäNtäsyôN
play	**la pièce de théâtre** lä pyes də tā·ät'rə
premiere	**la première** lä prəmyär
production	**la mise en scène** lä mēz äN sen
program	**le programme** lə prôgräm
seat	**la place** lä pläs
singer *(female)*	**la chanteuse** lä shäNtȩz
singer *(male)*	**le chanteur** lə shäNtȩr
soloist *(female)*	**la soliste** lä sôlēst
soloist *(male)*	**le soliste** lə sôlēst
subtitled	**sous-titré** sōō-tētrā
subtitles	**les sous-titres** *m/pl* lā sōō-tēt'rə
theater	**le théâtre** lə tā·ät'rə
ticket	**le billet d'entrée** lə bēye däNtrā
vaudeville show	**les variétés** *f/pl* lā väryätā

➡ *More Sports and Games (p. 183)*

GOING OUT IN THE EVENING

Is there a nice *bar/bistro* around here?	**Est-ce qu'il y a un bistrot sympathique par ici?** eskēlyä eN bēstrō seNpátēk pär ēsē?
Where can you go dancing around here?	**Où est-ce qu'on peut aller danser par ici?** ōō eskōN pä älā däNsä pär ēsē?
May I sit here?	**Cette place est encore libre?** set pläs etäNkôr lēb'rə?
Can you get something to eat here?	**Est-ce qu'on peut manger quelque chose ici?** eskōN pä mäNzhā kelkə shōz ēsē?

➡ Waiter! (p. 103)

Do you have a drinks menu?	**Est-ce que vous avez la carte des boissons?** eskə vōōzävā lä kärt dā bô·äsôN?
I'd like a *glass of wine/beer*, please.	***Un verre de vin/Une bière*, s'il vous plaît.** eN ver də veN/ēn byer, sēl vōō ple.
The same again, please.	**La même chose, s'il vous plaît.** lä mem shōz, sēl vōō ple.
What would you like to drink?	**Qu'est-ce que *vous voulez/tu veux* boire?** keskə vōō vōōlä/t̄ē və bô·är?

7

May I buy you a glass of wine?	**Est-ce que je peux *vous inviter/t'inviter* à prendre un verre de vin?** eskə zhə pä vōōzeNvētā/teNvētā ä präNd'rə eN ver də veN?
Would you like to dance?	**Je peux *vous inviter/t'inviter* pour cette danse?** zhə pä vōōzeNvētā/teNvētā pōōr set däNs?
You dance very well.	***Vous dansez/Tu danses* très bien.** vōō däNsā/tē däNs tre byeN.

 Small Talk (p. 19)

Going out in the Evening

available	**libre** lēb'rə
bar	**le bar** lə bär
bistro	**le bistrot** lə bēstrō
casino	**le casino** lə käsēnō
dance	**la danse** lä däNs
to dance	**danser** däNsā
disco	**la disco, la boîte** lä dēskō, lä bô·ät
to drink	**boire** bô·är
to invite	**inviter** eNvētā
loud	**bruyant** brēyäN

Post Office and Bank

POST, TELEGRAMS, TELEPHONE

Letters and Parcels

Where is the nearest *mailbox/post office*?	**Où est la *boîte aux lettres/poste* la plus proche?** ōō e lä bô·ät ō let'rə/pôst lä plē prôsh?
How much does a *letter/postcard* to America cost?	**Combien coûte une *lettre/carte* aux États-Unis?** kôNbyeN kōōt ēn let'rə/kärt ōzätäzēnē?
Five ... stamps, please.	**Cinq timbres à ..., s'il vous plaît.** seNk teNb'rə ä ..., sēl vōō ple.
Do you have any commemorative stamps?	**Est-ce que vous avez aussi des timbres spéciaux?** eskə vōōzävā ôsē dā teNb'rə spāsyō?
I'd like a set of each, please.	**Une série de chaque, s'il vous plaît.** ēn sārē də shäk, sēl vōō ple.
I'd like to mail this *letter/package* to ..., please.	***Cette lettre/Ce paquet ...,* s'il vous plaît.** set let'rə/sə päke ..., sēl vōō ple.
by airmail express by surface mail	**par avion** pär ävyôN **par exprès** pär ekspre **par voie ordinaire** pär vô·ä ôrdēner
I'd like to send a package.	**Je voudrais poster un colis.** zhə vōōdre pôstā eN kôlē.

194

Could you send a fax for me?	**Vous pouvez envoyer un fax pour moi?** vōō pōōvä äNvô-äyä eN fäks pōōr mô-ä?
Can I send a telegram here?	**Est-ce que je peux envoyer un télégramme à partir d'ici?** eskə zhə pä eNvô-äyä eN tälägräm ä pärter dēsē?
Please give me a form for a telegram.	**Donnez-moi un formulaire de télégramme, s'il vous plaît.** dônā-mô-ä eN fôrmēler də tälägräm, sēl vōō ple.
Where can I make a phone call?	**Où est-ce que je peux téléphoner ici?** ōō eskə zhə pä tälāfônä ēsē?
Could you tell me where I might find a phone booth?	**Vous pourriez m'indiquer une cabine téléphonique, s'il vous plaît?** vōō pōōryä meNdēkä ēn käbēn tälāfônēk, sēl vōō ple?

8

! **Prenez la cabine ...**   Go into booth ...
  prənā lä käbēn ...

INFO If you would like to use the public phones in France, it might be wise to buy a **télécarte** (telephone card), since most of the public phones in France are operated with one of these. The **télécarte** is a chip card loaded with a certain amount of money; you slip it into the phone before dialing. You can purchase a **télécarte** in most post offices, at newsstands and **bureaux de tabac** (tobacconist's) indicated by the sign **"Ici, vente de télécartes"**.

Excuse me, could you give me change to make a phone call?	**Excusez-moi, il me faudrait des pièces pour téléphoner.** ekskēzā-mô·ä, ēl mə fōdrā dā pyes pōōr tālāfônä.
Can you give me change for this bill?	**Vous pourriez me changer ce billet?** vōō pōōryā mə shäNzhā sə bēye?
What's the area code for ...?	**Quel est l'indicatif de ...?** kel e leNdēkätēf də ...?
Do you have a phone book for ...?	**Est-ce que vous avez un annuaire de ...?** eskə vōōzävā eNänē·er də ...?

INFO If you wish to phone America, dial "1" for the United States and Canada and then the area code and phone number with no further prefix.

! **La ligne est occupée.** lä lēn'ye etôkēpā.	The line is busy.
! **Ça ne répond pas.** sä nə räpôN pä.	There's no answer.
! **Essayez encore une fois.** esäyā äNkôr ēn fô·ä.	You'll have to try again.

When do evening rates apply?	**Le tarif de nuit est valable à partir de quelle heure?** lə tärēf də nē·ē e väläb'lə ä pärtēr də kelār?

address	**l'adresse** *f* lädres
addressee	**le destinataire** lə destēnäter
airmail	**par avion** pär ävyôN
area code	**l'indicatif** *m* leNdēkätēf
busy	**occupé** ôkēpā
to call (on the phone)	**téléphoner** tālāfônā
card-operated phone	**le téléphone à carte** lə tālāfôn ä kärt
C.O.D.	**contre remboursement** kôNt'rə räNbōōrsmäN
charge	**la taxe** lä täks
coin	**la pièce** lä pyes
collect call	**la communication en PCV** lä kômēnēkäsyôN äN pā-sā-vā
commemorative stamp	**le timbre spécial** lə teNb'rə späsyäl
to connect (a call)	**passer** päsā
counter	**le guichet** lə gēshe
customs declaration	**la déclaration de douane** lä dākläräsyôN də dōō-än
cut off	**coupé** kōōpā
declaration of value	**la valeur déclarée** lä välər dāklärā
evening rate	**le tarif de nuit** lə tärēf də nē-ē
express letter	**la lettre exprès** lä letrekspre
fax	**le (télé)fax** lə (tālā)fäks
international call	**la communication internationale** lä kômēnēkäsyôN eNternäsyônäl
letter	**la lettre** lä let'rə

8

197

mailbox	**la boîte aux lettres** lä bô·ät ō let'rə	
package	**le colis** lə kôlē	
– info form	**le bulletin d'expédition** lə bēlteN dekspädēsyôN	
parcel	**le paquet** lə päke	
pay phone	**le téléphone à pièces** lə tālāfôn ä pyes	
post office	**la poste** lä pôst	
postcard	**la carte postale** lä kärt pôstäl	
to send	**envoyer** äNvô·äyā	
sender	**l'expéditeur** *m* lekspādētär	
stamp	**le timbre** lə teNb'rə	
– vending machine	**le distributeur automatique de timbres** lə dēstrēbŭtär ôtômätēk də teNb'rə	
telegram	**le télégramme** lə tālāgräm	
telephone	**le téléphone** lə tālāfôn	
– booth	**la cabine téléphonique** lä käbēn tālāfônēk	
– card	**la télécarte** lä tālākärt	
– call	**la communication** lä kômēnēkäsyôN	
– directory	**l'annuaire** *m* länē·er	

MONEY MATTERS

Can you tell me where I can find a bank around here? | **Pardon, vous pourriez m'indiquer une banque dans le coin?** pärdôN, vōō pōōryā meNdēkä ēn bäNk däns lə kô-eN?

Where can I exchange foreign currency? | **Où est-ce que je peux changer de l'argent?** ōō eskə zhə pā shäNzhā də lärzhäN?

What's the commission charge? | **A combien s'élèvent les frais?** ä kôNbyeN sälev lā fre?

What time does the bank close? | **La banque est ouverte jusqu'à quelle heure?** lä bäNk etōōvert zhēskä kelär?

INFO Bank opening hours can vary widely. Banks are usually closed between noon and 2 p.m. And even if the bank is open, the window money-exchange might be closed. Banks are closed on Saturdays and Sundays. Some banks have countryside branches that are open only one, two, or three days a week.

8

I'd like to change ... dollars into euros. | **Je voudrais changer ... dollars en euros.** zhə vōōdre shäNzhā ... dôlär äN ārō'.

Someone is wiring me some money. Has it arrived yet? | **J'attends un virement télégraphique. Est-ce que l'argent est arrivé?** zhätäN eN vērmäN tālägräfēk. eskə lärzhäN etärēvä?

199

INFO In areas frequented by tourists you can find money-exchange bureaus either at the train station or at the tourist-information office (**syndicat d'initiative, office du tourisme**). They are also located at large highway rest stops and within the city of Paris. As with the banks, they all have differing opening hours. Exchange bureaus often have exorbitant exchange rates, so it might be wise to inquire about the rate before exchanging your money.

Can I use my credit card to get cash?	**Est-ce que je peux retirer de l'argent liquide avec ma carte de crédit?** eskə zhə pā rətērā də lärzhäN lēkēd ävek mä kärt də krädē?
I'd like to cash a traveler's check.	**Je voudrais encaisser un chèque de voyage.** zhə vōōdrə äNkesä eN shek də vô·äyäzh.
What's the highest amount I can cash?	**Quelle est la somme maximum?** kel ā lä sôm mäksēmôm?

?	**Vous avez une pièce d'identité sur vous, s'il vous plaît?** vōōzävā ēn pyes dēdäNtētā sēr vōō, sēl vōō ple?	May I see *your passport/some ID*, please?
!	**Une signature ici, s'il vous plaît.** ēn sēnyätēr ēsē, sēl vōō ple.	Would you sign here, please.
!	**Pour retirer l'argent, passez à la caisse, s'il vous plaît.** pōōr rətērā lärzhäN, päsā ä lä kes, sēl vōō ple.	You can pick up the money at the cashier.

200

? Vous le voulez comment?
vōō lə vōōlā kômäN?

How would you like the money?

In small bills, please.

Donnez-moi des petites coupures, s'il vous plaît. dônā-mô·ä dā pətēt kōōpēr, sēl vōō ple.

Please give me some change, too.

Donnez-moi aussi un peu de monnaie. dônā-mô·ä ôsē eN pə̄ də mône.

Money matters

amount	**le montant** lə môNtäN
ATM	**la billetterie** lä bēyetrē
bank	**la banque** lä bäNk
– account	**le compte en banque** lə kôNt äN bäNk
– code	**le code établissement** lə kôd ātäblēsmäN
– transfer	**le virement (bancaire)** lə vērmäN (bäNker)
bill	**le billet (de banque)** lə beye (də bäNk)
card number	**le numéro de la carte** lə nēmärō də lä kärt
cash	**l'argent** *m* **liquide** lärzhäN lēkēd
cashier	**la caisse** lä kes
change	**la monnaie** lä mône
check	**le chèque** lə shek
commission fee	**les frais** *m/pl* lā fre
counter	**le guichet** lə gēshe

8

201

credit card	**la carte de crédit** lä kärt də krādē
currency-exchange office	**le bureau de change** lə bē̲rō də shäNzh
to exchange *(money)*	**changer** shäNzhā
exchange rate	**le cours** lə kōōr
money	**l'argent** *m* lärzhäN
receipt	**la quittance** lä kētäNs
savings account	**le livret de caisse d'épargne** lə lēvre də kes däpärn'yə
to sign	**signer** sēnyā
signature	**la signature** lä sēnyätē̲r
traveler's check	**le chèque de voyage** lə shek də vô·äyäzh
to withdraw	**retirer** rətērā

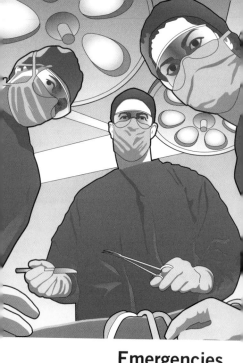

Emergencies

HEALTH

Information

Could you recommend a general practitioner?	**Est-ce que vous pouvez me recommander un médecin généraliste?** eskə vōō pōōvā mə rəkômäNdä eN mädseN zhänärälēst?
Does he speak English?	**Est-ce qu'il parle anglais?** eskēl pärl äNgle?
What are his office hours?	**Quelles sont ses heures de consultation?** kel sôN säzər də kôNsēltäsyôN?
Can he come here?	**Est-ce qu'il pourrait venir?** eskēl pōōre vənēr?
My *husband/wife* is sick.	***Mon mari/Ma femme* est malade.** môN märē/mä fäm e mäläd.

INFO S.A.M.U. sämē is the name of the emergency assistance you can reach anytime from anywhere in France by dialling the number "15." They will arrange for emergency services and ambulances. In an emergency you can also contact **les pompiers** lā pôNpyā (the fire department).

Please call *an ambulance/the emergency service!*	**Appelez *une ambulance/le S.A.M.U.*, s'il vous plaît.** äplā ēn äNbēläNs/lə sämē, sēl vōō ple.
Where are you taking *him/her?*	**Vous *le/la* transportez où?** vōō lə/lä träNspôrtā ōō?

| I'd like to come with you. | **Je voudrais venir avec.** zhə vōōdre vənēr ävek. |
| Where's the nearest (24-hour) pharmacy? | **Où est la pharmacie (de garde) la plus proche?** ōō e lä färmäsē (də gärd) lä plē prôsh? |

Drugstore

Do you have anything for ...?	**Vous avez quelque chose contre ...?** vōōzävä kelkə shōz kôNt'rə ...?
How should I take it?	**Comment est-ce que je dois le prendre?** kômäN eskə zhə dô·ä lə präNd'rə?
I need this medicine.	**J'ai besoin de ce médicament.** zhā bezô·eN də sə mädēkämäN.

	Ce médicament est uniquement délivré sur ordonnance. sə mädēkämäN etēnēkmäN dälēvrā sēr ôrdônäNs.	You need a prescription for this medicine.
!	**Nous ne l'avons pas en magasin.** nōō nə lävôN pä äN mägäzeN.	I'm sorry, but we don't have that here.
!	**Nous devons le commander.** nōō dəvôN lə kômäNdä.	We'll have to order it.

| When can I pick it up? | **Vous l'aurez quand?** vōō lôrā käN? |

9

205

Instructions

à jeun ä zhãN	on an empty stomach
après les repas äpre lā rəpä	after meals
avaler sans croquer ävälā säN krōkā	swallow whole
avant les repas äväN lā rəpä	before meals
conformément aux prescriptions du médecin kôNfôrməmäN ō preskrēpsyôN dē mädseN	according to the doctor's instructions
contre-indications kôNtreNdēkäsyôN	contraindications
effets secondaires efe səkôNder	side effects
externe ekstern	external
interne eNtern	internal
laisser fondre dans la bouche lāsā fôNd'rə däN lä bōōsh	to dissolve on the tongue
rectal rektäl	rectally
trois fois par jour trô·ä fô·ä pär zhōōr	three times a day

Drugstore

antibiotic	**l'antibiotique** *m* läNtēbē·ôtēk
antiseptic ointment	**la pommade cicatrisante** lä pômäd sēkätrēzäNt
bandages	**les pansements** *m/pl* lā päNsmäN
Band-Aid®	**le pansement** lə päNsmäN
(birth-control) pill	**la pilule contraceptive** lä pēlül kôNträseptēv
charcoal tablets	**des comprimés** *m/pl* **de charbon** dā kôNprēmā də shärbôN
condoms	**les préservatifs** *m/pl* lā prāservätēf

206

cotton	**le coton hydrophile** lə kôtôN idrôfēl
cough syrup	**le sirop contre la toux**
	lə sērō kôNt'rə lä tōō
disinfectant	**le désinfectant** lə däzeNfektäN
drops	**les gouttes** *f/pl* lā gōōt
drugstore	**la pharmacie** lä färmäsē
elastic bandage	**la bande élastique** lä bäNd älästēk
gauze bandage	**la bande de gaze** lä bäNd də gäz
homeopathic	**homéopathique** ômā-ôpätēk
injection	**la piqûre** lä pēkę̄r
iodine	**l'iode** *m* lyôd
laxative	**le laxatif** lə läksätēf
medicine to improve	**le médicament pour la circulation du**
blood circulation	**sang** lə mādēkämäN pōōr lä
	sērkäläsyôN dē̩ säN
medicine to reduce	**le fébrifuge** lə fābrēfē̩zh
fever	
night duty	**la garde de nuit** lä gärd də nē̩-ē
ointment	**la pommade** lä pômäd
– for mosquito	**la pommade contre les piqûres de**
bites	**moustiques** lä pômäd kôNt'rə lā
	pēkę̄r də mōōstēk
– for sunburn	**la pommade contre les coups de**
	soleil lä pômäd kôNt'rə lä kōō də
	sôle'ē
painkiller	**l'analgésique** *m* länälzhāzēk
prescription	**l'ordonnance** *f* lôrdônäNs
sanitary napkin	**la serviette hygiénique**
	lä servyet ēzhē-änēk

9

207

sleeping pills	**le somnifère** lə sômnēfer
something for ...	**le remède contre ...** lə rəmed kôNt'rə

➡ *Diseases, Doctor, Hospital (p. 217)*

suppository	**le suppositoire** lə sēpôzētô·är
tablets for ...	**les comprimés** *m/pl* **contre ...**
	lā kôNprēmā kôNt'rə ...
tampons	**les tampons** *m/pl* lā täNpôN
thermometer	**le thermomètre médical**
	lə termōmet'rə mādēkäl
tranquilizer	**le calmant** lə kälmäN

At the Doctor's

I have a (bad) cold.	**J'ai un (gros) rhume.**
	zhā eN (grō) rēm.
I have *diarrhea/a* *fever*.	**J'ai la *diarrhée/fièvre*.**
	zhā lä *dyärā/fyev'rə*.
I'm constipated.	**Je suis constipé.**
	zhə svē kôNstēpā.
My ... *hurts/hurt*.	**J'ai mal *à/aux* ...** zhā mäl *ä/ō* ...

➡ *Parts of the Body and Organs (p. 215)*

I have pains here.	**J'ai mal ici.** zhā mäl ēsē.

INFO Doctors in France are addressed simply as **"Docteur"** dôktār without **Monsieur** məsyā, **Madame** mädäm or last name. Make sure you bring your health-insurance information with you.

I've been vomiting (a lot).	**J'ai vomi (plusieurs fois).** zhā vômē (plēsyär fô·ä).
My stomach is upset.	**J'ai un embarras d'estomac.** zhā eNäNbärä destômä.
I can't move ...	**Je ne peux pas bouger ...** zhə nə pā pä bōōzhā ...

➡ *Parts of the Body and Organs (p. 215)*

I've hurt myself.	**Je me suis blessé.** zhə mə svē blesā.
I had a fall.	**Je suis tombé.** zhə svē tôNbā.
I've been *stung/bitten* by ...	**J'ai été *piqué/mordu* par ...** zhā ätā *pēkā/môrdē* pär ...

What you should tell the Doctor

I have (not) been vaccinated against ...	**Je (ne) suis (pas) vacciné contre ...** zhə (nə) svē (pä) väksēnā kôNt'rə ...
My last tetanus shot was about ... years ago.	**Ma dernière vaccination contre le tétanos remonte à ... ans environ.** mä dernyer väksēnäsyôN kôNt'rə lə tātänôs rəmôNt ä ... äN äNvērôN.
I'm allergic to penicillin.	**Je suis allergique à la pénicilline.** zhə svē älerzhēk ä lä pānēsēlēn.
I have *high/low* blood pressure.	**Je souffre *d'hypertension/d'hypotension*.** zhə sōōf'rə *dēpertäNsyôN/ dēpôtäNsyôN.*
I have a pacemaker.	**Je porte un stimulateur (cardiaque).** zhə pôrt eN stēmēlätār (kärdyäk).
I'm four months pregnant.	**Je suis enceinte de quatre mois.** zhə svē äNseNt də kät'rə mô·ä.
I'm diabetic.	**Je suis diabétique.** zhə svē dyäbātēk.
I'm HIV-positive.	**Je suis ♂ séropositif/♀ séropositive.** zhə svē ♂ sārôpōzētēf/♀ sārôpōzētēv.
I take this medicine regularly.	**Je prends régulièrement ces médicaments.** zhə präN rāgēlyermäN sā mādēkämäN.

What the Doctor says

Qu'est-ce que vous avez comme problèmes? keskə vōōzávā kôm prôblem?

What are your symptoms?

Où avez-vous mal? ōō ávā-vōō mäl?

Where does it hurt?

Ici, vous avez mal? ēsē, vōōzávā mäl?

Does this hurt?

Ouvrez la bouche. ōōvrā lä bōōsh.

Open your mouth.

Montrez la langue. môNtrā lä läNg.

Show me your tongue.

Toussez. tōōsā.

Cough.

Déshabillez-vous, s'il vous plaît. dāzäbēyā-vōō, sēl vōō ple.

Would you get undressed, please.

Relevez votre manche, s'il vous plaît. relvā vôt'rə mäNsh, sēl vōō ple.

Would you roll up your sleeve, please.

Inspirez profondément. Ne respirez plus. ēNspērā prôfôNdəmäN. nə respērā plē.

Breathe deeply. Now hold your breath.

Depuis quand avez-vous ces problèmes? dəpē-ē käN ávā-vōō sā prôblem?

How long have you felt this way?

Est-ce que vous êtes vacciné contre ...? eskə vōōzet väksēnā kôNt'rə ...?

Have you been vaccinated against ...?

9

211

Nous devons vous faire une radio.
noo dəvôN voo fer ẹn rädyō.

We need to take some X-rays.

Vous avez une *fracture/entorse* de ...
voozävä ẹn fräktẹr/äNtôrs də ...

Your ... is *broken/sprained.*

Il faut faire une analyse *de sang/d'urine*. ẹl fō fer ẹn änälēz də säN/dẹrẹn.

We need to take a *blood/urine* sample.

Il faut vous opérer. ẹl fō voozôpārā.

You'll have to have an operation.

Je dois vous envoyer chez un spécialiste. zhə dô·ä voozäNvô·äyā shā eN spāsyälēst.

I'll have to refer you to a specialist.

Ce n'est rien de grave.
se ne rē·eN də gräv.

It's nothing serious.

Vous en prendrez ... *comprimés/gouttes* ... fois par jour. voozäN präNdrā ... kôNprēmā/goot ... fô·ä pär zhoor.

Take ... *tablets/drops* ... times a day.

Revenez *demain/dans ... jours*.
revnā dəmeN/däN ... zhoor.

Come back *tomorrow/in ... days.*

212

Ask the Doctor

Is it serious?

C'est grave? se gräv?

Can you give me a doctor's certificate?

Est-ce que vous pourriez me faire un certificat? eskə vōō pōōryā mə fer eN sertēfēkä?

Do I have to come back again?

Est-ce que je dois revenir? eskə zhə dô·ä revnēr?

What precautions should I take?

Quelles précautions dois-je prendre? kel präkôsyôN dô·äzh präNd'rə?

Could you give me a receipt (in English) for my medical insurance?

Pourriez-vous me donner une quittance (en anglais) pour mon assurance, s'il vous plaît? pōōryā-vōō mə dônā ēn kētäNs (änäNgle) pōōr mônäsēräNs, sēl vōō ple?

In the Hospital

Is there anyone here who speaks English?

Est-ce qu'il y a ici quelqu'un qui parle anglais? eskēlyä ēsē kelkeN kē pärl äNgle?

I'd like to speak to a doctor.

Je voudrais parler à un médecin. zhə vōōdre pärlā ä eN mädseN.

➡ *At the Doctor's (p. 208)*

What's the diagnosis?

Quel est le diagnostic? kel e lə dyägnôstēk?

9

I'd rather have the operation in the U.S.	**Je préfère me faire opérer aux Etats-Unis.** zhə präfer mə fer ôpārā ōzātäzēnē.
I'm insured for the journey home to the U.S.	**Mon assurance couvre les frais de rapatriement aux États-Unis.** mônäsēräNs kōōv'rə lä fre də räpätrēmäN ōzātäzēnē.
Would you please notify my family?	**Prévenez ma famille, s'il vous plaît.** prävnā mä fämē'ē, sēl vōō ple.
Here's the *address/ telephone number*.	**Voici *l'adresse/le numéro de téléphone*.** vô·äsē *lädres/lə nēmārō də tālāfón*.
How long will I have to stay here?	**Je dois rester ici encore combien de temps?** zhə dô·ä restā ēsē äNkôr kôNbyeN də täN?
When can I get out of bed?	**Quand est-ce que je pourrai me l ever?** käNdeskə zhə pōōrā mə ləvā?
Could you give me *something for the pain/to go to sleep*?	**Donnez-moi quelque chose *contre la douleur/pour dormir*, s'il vous plaît.** dônā-mô·ä kelkə shōz *kôN'rə lä dōōlär/ pōōr dôrmēr*, sēl vōō ple.
I'd like to be dis-charged. (I'll assume full responsibility.)	**Je voudrais sortir de l'hôpital. (C'est à mes risques et périls.)** zhə vōōdre sôrtēr də lôpētäl. (setä mä rēsk ā pārēl.)

Parts of the Body and Organs

abdomen	**le ventre** lə väNt're
ankle	**la cheville** lä shəve'ē
appendix	**l'appendice** *m* läpäNdēs
arm	**le bras** lə brä
back	**le dos** lə dō
bladder	**la vessie** lä vesē
bone	**l'os** *m* lôs
chest	**la poitrine** lä pô·ätrēn
collarbone	**la clavicule** lä klävekēl
(intervertebral) disk	**le disque intervertébral** lə dēsk eNtervertäbräl
ear	**l'oreille** *f* lôre'ē
-drum	**le tympan** lə teNpäN
eye	**l'œil** *m, pl:* **les yeux** lā'ē, *pl:* lāzyā
finger	**le doigt** lə dô·ä
foot	**le pied** lə pyä
forehead	**le front** lə frôN
gallbladder	**la bile** lä bēl
hand	**la main** lä meN
head	**la tête** lä tet
heart	**le cœur** lə kār
hip	**la hanche** lä äNsh
intestines	**les intestins** *m/pl* läzeNtesteN
joint	**l'articulation** *f* lärtēkēläsyôN
kidney	**le rein** lə reN
knee	**le genou** lə zhənōō
-cap	**la rotule** lä rôtēl
leg	**la jambe** lä zhäNb

9

215

liver	**le foie** lə fôˑä
lungs	**les poumons** *m/pl* lā pōōmôN
mouth	**la bouche** lä bōōsh
muscle	**le muscle** lə mēsk'lə
neck *(in general)*	**le cou** lə kōō
neck *(nape)*	**la nuque** lä nēk
nerve	**le nerf** lə ner
nose	**le nez** lə nā
penis	**le pénis** lə pānēs
rib	**la côte** lä kôt
shoulder	**l'épaule** *f* lāpōl
sinus	**le sinus frontal** lə sēnēs frôNtäl
skin	**la peau** lä pō
spine	**la colonne vertébrale** lä kôlôn vertābräl
stomach	**l'estomac** *m* lestōmä
temple	**la tempe** lä täNp
tendon	**le tendon** lə täNdôN
thigh	**la cuisse** lä kēˑēs
throat	**la gorge** lä gôrzh
thyroid	**la thyroïde** lä tērôˑēd
toe	**l'orteil** *m* lôrte'ē
tongue	**la langue** lä läNg
tooth	**la dent** lä däN
torso	**le haut du corps** lə ō dē̱ kôr
vagina	**le vagin** lə väzheN
vertebra	**la vertèbre** lä verteb'rə

AIDS	**le sida** lə sēdä
allergy	**l'allergie** *f* lälerzhē
appendicitis	**l'appendicite** *f* läpäNdēsēt
asthma	**l'asthme** *m* läsm
bite	**la morsure** lä môrsēr
bleeding	**le saignement** lə senyəmäN
blister	**l'ampoule** *f* läNpōōl
blood	**le sang** lə säN
blood poisoning	**l'empoisonnement** *m* du sang läNpô·äsônmäN dē säN
blood pressure	**la tension (sanguine)** lä täNsyôN (säNgēn)
high –	**l'hypertension** *f* lēpertäNsyôN
low –	**l'hypotension** *f* lēpôtäNsyôN
blood transfusion	**la transfusion de sang** lä träNsfēzyôN də säN
blood type	**le groupe sanguin** lə grōōp säNgeN
broken	**cassé** käsā
bruise	**la contusion** lä kôNtēzyôN
burn	**la brûlure** lä brēlēr
cardiac arrest	**l'infarctus** *m* leNfärktēs
(plaster) cast	**le plâtre** lə plät'rə
(doctor's) certificate	**le certificat (médical)** lə sertēfēkä (mādēkäl)
chicken pox	**la varicelle** lä värēsel
circulation problems	**les troubles** *m/pl* **circulatoires** lā trōōb'lə sērkēlätô·är

colic	**la colique** lä kôlēk
concussion	**la commotion cérébrale** lä kômôsyôN säräbräl
conjunctivitis	**la conjonctivite** lä kôNzhôNktēvēt
constipation	**la constipation** lä kôNstēpäsyôN
contagious	**contagieux** kôNtäzhyä
cough	**la toux** lä tōō
cramp	**la crampe** lä kräNp
cystitis	**la cystite** lä sēstēt
dermatologist	**le dermatologue** lə dermätôlôg
diabetes	**le diabète** lə dyäbet
diarrhea	**la diarrhée** lä dyärä
dislocated	**luxé** lēksä
dizziness	**les vertiges** *m/pl* lā vertēzh
doctor *(male)*	**le médecin** lə mādseN
doctor *(female)*	**la femme médecin** lä fäm mādseN
ear infection	**l'otite** *f* lōtēt
ear, nose, and throat doctor (ENT)	**l'oto-rhino-laryngologiste** *m* lôtô-rēnō-läreNgôlôzhēst
to faint	**s'évanouir** sāvänōō-ēr
fever	**la fièvre** lä fyev'rə
flu	**la grippe** lä grēp
food poisoning	**l'intoxication** *f* **alimentaire** leNtôksēkäsyôN älēmäNter
fungal infection	**la mycose** lä mēkôz
gallstones	**le calcul biliaire** lə kälkēl bēlyer
general practitioner	**le médecin généraliste** lə mādseN zhānārälēst
German measles	**la rubéole** lä rēbā-ôl

218

gynecologist *(male/female)*	*le/la* **gynécologue** lə/lä zhēnākôlôg
hay fever	**le rhume des foins** lə rēm dā fô·eN
headache	**le mal de tête** lə mäl də tet
heart	**le cœur** lə kēr
– attack	**la crise cardiaque** lä krēz kärdyäk
– defect	**l'anomalie** *f* **cardiaque** länômälē kärdyäk
hernia	**la hernie** lä ernē
herpes	**l'herpès** *m* lerpes
hospital	**l'hôpital** *m* lôpētäl
infection	**l'infection** *f* leNfeksyôN
inflammation	**l'inflammation** *f* leNflämäsyôN
injury	**la blessure** lä blesēr
internist	**le spécialiste des maladies internes** lə spāsyälēst dā mälädē eNtern
kidney stones	**les calculs** *m/pl* **rénaux** lā kälkēl rānō
lumbago	**le lumbago** lə lôNbägō
measles	**la rougeole** lä rōōzhôl
menstruation	**la menstruation** lä mäNstrē·äsyôN
migraine	**la migraine** lä mēgren
mumps	**les oreillons** *m/pl* läzôrāyôN
nausea	**les nausées** *f/pl* lā nōzā
nosebleed	**les saignements** *m/pl* **de nez** lā senyəmäN də nā
office hours	**les heures** *f/pl* **de consultation** lāzēr də kôNsēltäsyôN

9

219

to operate on	**opérer** ôpārā
ophthalmologist	**l'oculiste** *m* lôkēlēst
orthopedist	**l'orthopédiste** *m* lôrtôpādēst
pacemaker	**le stimulateur (cardiaque)**
	lə stēmēlätär (kärdyäk)
pain(s)	**les douleurs** *f/pl* lā dōōlär
pediatrician	**le pédiatre** lə pädyät'rə
pneumonia	**la pneumonie** lä pnəmônē
pregnant	**enceinte** äNseNt
to prescribe	**prescrire** preskrēr
pulled ligament	**l'élongation** lälôNgäsyôN
pulled muscle	**le claquage musculaire**
	lə kläkäzh mēskēler
pulled tendon	**l'élongation** *f* lälôNgäsyôN
pus	**le pus** lə pē
rheumatism	**les rhumatismes** lə rēmätēsm
scarlet fever	**la scarlatine** lä skärlätēn
shivering	**les frissons** *m/pl* lā frēsôN
shock	**le choc** lə shôk
sore throat	**le mal de gorge** lə mäl də gôrzh
sprained	**foulé** fōōlā
sting	**la piqûre** lä pēkēr
stomachache	**le mal d'estomac** lə mäl destômä
stroke	**l'attaque** *f* **(d'apoplexie)**
	lätäk (däpôpleksē)
sunstroke	**l'insolation** *f* leNsôläsyôN
sunburn	**le coup de soleil** lə kōō də sôle'ē
sweating	**les sueurs** *f/pl* lā sē-är
swelling	**l'enflure** *f* läNflēr

tetanus	**le tétanos** lə tātänôs
tick	**la tique** lä tēk
torn ligament	**la déchirure** lä dāshērēr
ulcer *(stomach)*	**l'ulcère** *m* **d'estomac** lēlser destôma
urine analysis	**l'analyse** *f* **d'urines** länälēz dērēn
urologist	**l'urologue** *m* lērôlôg
vaccination	**la vaccination** lä väksēnäsyôN
– record	**le carnet de vaccination** lə kärne də väksēnäsyôN
veterinarian	**le vétérinaire** lə vātārēner
vomiting	**les vomissements** *m/pl* lā vômēsmäN
ward	**le service** lə servēs
to X-ray	**faire une radio** fer ēn rädyō

At the Dentist's

This tooth hurts.	**J'ai mal à cette dent.** zhā mäl ä set däN.
This tooth is broken.	**La dent s'est cassée.** lä däN se käsā.
I've lost a filling.	**J'ai perdu un plomb.** zhā perdē eN plôN.
Can you do a temporary job on my tooth?	**Est-ce que vous pourriez soigner la dent de façon provisoire?** eskə vōō pōōryā sô·änyā lä däN də fäsôN prôvēzô·är?

9

Please don't pull the tooth.	**Je ne veux pas que vous m'arrachiez la dent.** zhə nə vä pä kə vōō märäshyā lä däN.
Would you give me/ I'd rather not have an injection, please.	***Faites-moi une injection/Ne me faites pas d'injection,** s'il vous plaît.* fet-mô·ä ēn eNzheksyôN/nə mə fet pä deNzheksyôN, sēl vōō ple.

What the Dentist says

Vous avez besoin ...
vōōzävā bəzô·eN ...

d'un bridge. deN brēdzh.	bridge.
d'un plombage. deN plôNbäzh.	filling.
d'une couronne. dēn kōōrôn.	crown.

Je dois extraire la dent.
zhə dô·ä ekstrer lä däN.

I'll have to pull the tooth.

Rincez bien. reNsā byeN.

Rinse out your mouth.

Ne rien manger pendant deux heures, s'il vous plaît. nə rē·eN mäNzhā päNdäN dāzār, sēl vōō ple.

Don't eat anything for two hours.

At the Dentist's

amalgam	**l'amalgame** *m* lämälgäm
bridge	**le bridge** lə brēdzh
cavity	**la carie** lä kärē

crown	**la couronne** lä kōōrôn
gold –	**la couronne en or** lä kōōrôn änôr
porcelain –	**la couronne en porcelaine** lä kōōrôn äN pôrsələn
dentist	**le dentiste** lə däNtēst
dentures	**le dentier** lə däNtyā
filling	**le plombage** lə plôNbäzh
temporary –	**le traitement provisoire** lə tretmäN prôvēzô·är
gums	**la gencive** lä zhäNsēv
imprint	**l'empreinte** *f* läNpreNt
infection	**l'inflammation** *f* leNflämäsyôN
injection	**l'injection** *f* leNzheksyôN
jaw	**la mâchoire** lä mäshô·är
local anesthetic	**l'anesthésie** *f* **locale** länestāzē lôkäl
nerve	**le nerf** lə ner
to pull *(a tooth)*	**arracher** äräshā
pyorrhea	**la parodontose** lä pärädôntöz
root	**la racine** lä räsēn
-canal work	**le traitement de la racine** lə tretmäN də lä räsēn
tooth	**la dent** lä däN
wisdom –	**la dent de sagesse** lä däN də säzhes

9

POLICE; LOST AND FOUND

Where is the nearest police station?	**Où est le poste de police le plus proche?** ōō e lə pôst də pôlēs lə plē prôsh?
Does anyone here speak English?	**Est-ce qu'il y a ici quelqu'un qui parle anglais?** eskēlyä ēsē kelkeN kē pärl äNgle?
I'd like to report a theft.	**Je voudrais déposer une plainte pour vol.** zhə vōōdre dāpōzā ēn pleNt pōōr vôl.
I'd like to report an accident.	**Je voudrais faire une déclaration d'accident.** zhə vōōdre fer ēn dāklärāsyôN däksēdäN.

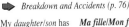 *Breakdown and Accidents (p. 76)*

My *daughter/son* has disappeared.	**Ma fille/Mon fils a disparu.** mä fē'ē/môN fēs ä dēspärē.
My ... has been stolen.	**On m'a volé ...** ôN mä vôlā ...
I've lost ...	**J'ai perdu ...** zhā perdē ...
My car has been broken into.	**On a ouvert ma voiture par effraction.** ôNä ōōver mä vô·tēr pär efräksyôN.
My *house/room* has been broken into.	**On a cambriolé ma *maison/chambre*.** ôNä käNbrē·ôlā mä *mezôN/shäNb'rə*.
I need a copy of the official report for insurance purposes.	**J'ai besoin d'une attestation pour mon assurance.** zhā bezô·eN dēn ätestäsyôN pōōr môNäsēräNs.

224

I'd like to speak to *my lawyer/the consulate*.	**Je voudrais parler *à mon avocat/avec mon consulat.*** zhə vōōdre pärlä ä mônävôkä/ävek môN kôNsēlä.
I'm innocent.	**Je suis ♂ innocent/♀ innocente.** zhə svē ♂ ēnôsäN/♀ ēnôsäNt.

What the Police say

Remplissez ce formulaire. räNplēsā sə fôrmēler.	Please fill out this form.
Votre passeport, s'il vous plaît. vôt'rə päspôr, sēl vōō ple.	Your passport, please.
Quelle est votre adresse aux États-Unis? kel e vôträdres ōzätäzēnē?	What is your address in America?
Où habitez-vous ici? ōō äbētā-vōō ēsē?	Where are you staying here?
***Quand/Où* est-ce que c'est arrivé?** *käN/ōō* eskə setärēvä?	*When/Where* did this happen?
Contactez votre consulat, s'il vous plaît. kôNtäktā vôt'rə kôNsēlä, sēl vōō ple.	Please get in touch with your consulate.

9

225

accident	**l'accident** *m* läksēdäN
to arrest	**arrêter** ärätā
to break into	**cambrioler** käNbrē·ôlā
car	**la voiture** lä vô·ätēr
– radio	**l'autoradio** *m* lôtôrädyō
– registration	**les papiers** *m/pl* **de voiture** lā päpyā də vô·ätēr
consulate	**le consulat** lə kôNsēlä
handbag	**le sac à main** lə säk ä meN
to harass	**importuner** eNpôrtēnā
ID	**la carte d'identité** lä kärt dēdäNtētā
lawyer	**l'avocat** *m* lävôkä
lost	**perdu** perdē
lost and found	**le bureau des objets trouvés** lə bērō dāzôbzhe trōōvā
mugging	**l'agression** *f* lägresyôN
passport	**le passeport** lə päspôr
police	**la police** lä pôlēs
– officer	**le policier** lə pôlēsyā
– station	**le poste de police** lə pôst də pôlēs
to press charges	**porter plainte** pôrtā pleNt
rape	**le viol** lə vyôl
stolen	**volé** vôlā
theft	**le vol** lə vôl
thief	**le voleur** lə vôlēr
wallet	**le porte-monnaie** lə pôrt-mône
witness	**le témoin** lə tāmô·eN

Time and Weather

TIME

Time of Day

What time is it?	**Quelle heure est-il?** kelār etēl?
It's one o'clock.	**Il est une heure.** ēletēnār.
It's two o'clock.	**Il est deux heures.** ēl e dāzār.
It's three thirty-five.	**Il est quinze heures trente-cinq.** ēl e keNzār trāNt-seNk.
It's a quarter past five.	**Il est cinq heures et quart.** ēl e keNzār ā kär.
It's six-thirty.	**Il est six heures et demie.** ēl e sēsār ā dəmē.
It's a quarter to nine.	**Il est neuf heures moins le quart.** ēl e nēfār mô-eN lə kär.
It's five after four.	**Il est quatre heures cinq.** ēl e kätrār seNk.
It's ten to eight.	**Il est huit heures moins dix.** ēl e ē̄-ētār mô-eN dēs.
(At) What time?	**A quelle heure?** ä kelār?
At ten o'clock.	**A dix heures.** ä dēsār.
Around eleven.	**Vers onze heures.** ver ôNzār.
Nine o'clock sharp.	**A neuf heures trente précises.** ä nāfār trāNt prāsēz.

From eight till nine (o'clock).	**De huit heures à neuf heures.** də ē-ētär à nāfär.
Between ten and twelve.	**Entre dix et douze.** äNt'rə dēs ā dōōz.
Not before seven p.m.	**Pas avant dix-neuf heures.** päsäväN dēs-nāfär.
Just after nine o'clock.	**Un peu après neuf heures.** eN pā äpre nāfär.
In half an hour.	**Dans une demi-heure.** däNzēn dəmē-är.
In two hours.	**Dans deux heures.** däN dāzär.
It's (too) late.	**Il est (trop) tard.** ēl e (trō) tär.
It's still too early.	**Il est encore trop tôt.** ēl etäNkôr trō tō.

Basic Vocabulary

afternoon	**l'après-midi** *m* läpre-mēdē
in the –	**l'après-midi** *m* läpre-mēdē
this –	**cet après-midi** setäpre-mēdē
ago	**il y a** ēlyä
before	**avant** äväN
day	**le jour** lə zhōōr
every –	**tous les jours** tōō lā zhōōr
earlier	**plus tôt** plē tō
early	**tôt** tō
evening	**le soir** lə sô·àr

10

229

in the –	**le soir** lə sô·är
this –	**ce soir** sə sô·är
every week	**chaque semaine** shäk səmēn
hour	**l'heure** *f* lär
every –	**toutes les heures** tōōt läzär
half an –	**la demi-heure** lä dəmē-är
quarter of an –	**le quart d'heure** lə kär där
late	**tard** tär
later	**plus tard** plē tär
minute	**la minute** lä mēnēt
month	**le mois** lə mô·ä
morning	**le matin** lə mäteN
in the –	**le matin** lə mätəN
this –	**ce matin** sə mäteN
night	**la nuit** lä nē·ē
at –	**la nuit** lä nē·ē
last –	**hier soir** yer sô·är
noon	**midi** mēdē
at –	**à midi** ä mēdē
at – today	**ce midi** sə mēdē
now	**maintenant** meNtnäN
recently	**récemment** rāsämäN
since	**depuis** dəpē·ē
sometimes	**quelquefois** kelkəfô·ä
soon	**bientôt** byeNtō
time	**le temps** lə täN
in/on –	**à temps** ä täN
today	**aujourd'hui** ōzhōōrdvē
tomorrow	**demain** dəmeN

230

the day after –	**après-demain** äpre-dəmeN
tonight	**cette nuit, ce soir** set nē̇-ē̇, sə sô·är
until	**jusqu'à** zhēskä
week	**la semaine** lä səmen
in two weeks	**dans quinze jours** däN keNz zhōōr
weekend	**le week-end** lə ōō·ēk-end
on the –	**le week-end** lə ōō·ēk-end
year	**l'année** *f* länā
last –	**l'année** *f* **dernière** länā dernyer
next –	**l'année** *f* **prochaine** länā prôshen
yesterday	**hier** yer
the day before –	**avant-hier** äväNtyer

Seasons

spring	**le printemps** lə preNtäN
summer	**l'été** *m* lātā
fall	**l'automne** *m* lôtôn
winter	**l'hiver** *m* lēver

Legal Holidays

All Saints' Day	**la Toussaint** lä tōōseN
Christmas	**Noël** nô·el
Christmas Eve	**la veille de Noël** lä ve'ē̇ də nô·el
Easter	**Pâques** päk
Mardi gras	**le carnaval** lə kärnäväl
New Year	**le jour de l'an** lə zhōōr də läN
New Year's Eve	**la Saint-Sylvestre** lä seN-sēlvest'rə

10

INFO Bastille Day on July 14 is a national holiday in France. It is celebrated with parades and dances in the evening. Other holidays include May 8 (the end of World War II) and November 11 (Armistice Day, end of World War I).

THE DATE

What's today's date?	**On est le combien aujourd'hui?** ôNe lə kôNbyeN ōzhōōrdvē?
Today is July 2.	**Aujourd'hui, on est le deux juillet.** ōzhōōrdvē, ôNe lə dä zhē-ēye.
I was born on August 24, 1971.	**Je suis né le vingt-quatre août 1971.** zhə svē nā lə veN-kätrōōt mēl näf säN sô-äsäNtä-eN.
On the 4th of *this/next* month.	**Le quatre** *de ce mois/du mois pro-chain.* lə kät'rə də sə mô-ä/dē mô-ä prôsheN.
Until March 10.	**Jusqu'au dix mars.** zhēskō dē märs.
We're leaving on August 20.	**Nous partons le vingt août.** nōō pärtôN lə veNtōōt.
We arrived on July 25.	**Nous sommes arrivés le vingt-cinq juillet.** nōō sôm ärēvā lə veN-seNk zhē-ēye.

232

Days of the Week

Monday	**lundi** leNdē
Tuesday	**mardi** märdē
Wednesday	**mercredi** merkrədē
Thursday	**jeudi** zhādē
Friday	**vendredi** väNdrədē
Saturday	**samedi** sämdē
Sunday	**dimanche** dēmäNsh

Months

January	**janvier** zhäNvyā
February	**février** fāvrē·ā
March	**mars** märs
April	**avril** ävrēl
May	**mai** me
June	**juin** zhē·eN
July	**juillet** zhē·ēye
August	**août** ōot
September	**septembre** septäNb're
October	**octobre** ôktôb're
November	**novembre** nôväNb're
December	**décembre** dāsäNb're

THE WEATHER

What's the weather going to be like today?	**Quel temps va-t-il faire aujourd'hui?** kel täN vätēl fer ōzhōōrdvē?
Have you heard the weather forecast?	**Vous avez déjà écouté la météo?** vōōzävā dāzhä äkōōtā lä mātā-ō?
It's going to be/get ...	**Il fait/va faire ...** ēl fe/vä fer ...

warm.	**chaud.** shō.
hot.	**très chaud.** tre shō.
cold.	**froid.** frô-ä.
cool.	**frais.** fre.
humid.	**lourd.** lōōr.

It's rather windy.	**Il y a pas mal de vent.** ēlyä pä mäl də väN.
It's very windy.	**Il y a de la tempête.** ēlyä də lä täNpet.
What's the temperature?	**Quelle est la température?** kel e lä täNpärätēr?
It's ... degrees above/below zero.	**Il fait ... degrés au-dessus/au-dessous de zéro.** ēl fe ... dəgrä ōdəsē/ōdəsōō də zärō.
It looks like rain/a storm.	**On dirait qu'il va pleuvoir/faire de l'orage.** ôN dēre kēl vä plœvô-är/fer də lôräzh.

Weather

air	**l'air** *m* ler
blizzard	**la tempête de neige** lä täNpāt də nezh
clear	**clair** kler
climate	**le climat** lə klēmä
cloud	**le nuage** lə nē·äzh
cold	**froid** frô·ä
I'm –	**j'ai froid** zhā frô·ä
cool	**frais,** *f:* **fraîche** fre, *f.* fresh
degree	**le degré** lə dəgrā
dry	**sec,** *f:* **sèche** sek, *f.* sesh
fair *(weather)*	**beau** bō
fog	**le brouillard** lə brōōyär
it's freezing	**il gèle** ēl zhel
frost	**le gel** lə zhel
it's hailing	**il grêle** ēl grel
hazy	**brumeux** brēmə
heat	**la grosse chaleur** lä grôs shälər
high-pressure area	**l'anticyclone** *m* läNtēsēklôn
hot	**chaud** shō
I'm –	**j'ai chaud** zhā shō
humid	**humide** ēmēd
ice *(on the roads)*	**le verglas** lə verglä
lightning	**les éclairs** *m/pl* lāzāklēr
low-pressure area	**la dépression** lä dāpresyôN
moon	**la lune** lä lēn
overcast	**nuageux** nē·äzhə
precipitation	**les précipitations** *f/pl* lā prāsēpētäsyôN
rain	**la pluie** lä plē·ē

10

235

it's raining	**il pleut** ēl plə̄
shower *(of rain)*	**l'averse** *f* lävers
snow	**la neige** lä nezh
it's snowing	**il neige** ēl nezh
star	**l'étoile** *f* lātô·äl
storm	**la tempête** lä täNpet
it's stormy	**il y a de la tempête** ēlyä də lä täNpet
sultry *(weather)*	**lourd** lōōr
sun	**le soleil** lə sôle'ē
sunny	**ensoleillé** äNsôlāyā
sunrise	**le lever du soleil** lə ləvā dē sôle'ē
sunset	**le coucher du soleil** lə kōōshā dē sôle'ē
temperature	**la température** lä täNpārätēr
thaw	**le dégel** lə dāzhel
it's thawing	**c'est le dégel** se lə dāzhel
it's thundering	**il tonne** ēl tôn
thunderstorm	**l'orage** *m* lôräzh
variable	**capricieux** käprēsyə̄
warm	**chaud** shō
weather	**le temps** lə täN
– forecast	**la météo** lä mātā·ō
wet	**mouillé** mōōyā
wind	**le vent** lə väN
– strength	**la force du vent** lä fôrs dē väN
it's windy	**il y a du vent** ēlyä dē väN

Grammar

ARTICLES

Definite and Indefinite Articles

As with most other foreign languages, French divides nouns into genders: nouns and their preceding articles are either *masculine* or *feminine*.

	Singular		Plural	
	♂	♀	♂	♀
Definite Article	**le jour** the day	**la nuit** the night	**les jours** the days	**les nuits** the nights
Indefinite Article	**un jour** a day	**une nuit** a night	**des jours** days	**des nuits** nights

When followed by a word starting with a vowel or the silent **h**, the articles **le** and **la** abbreviate into **l'**: **l'avion** – the airplane, **l'adresse** – the address, **l'hotel** – the hotel.

When used together with the prepositions **à** and **de**, the articles **le** and **les** contract as follows:

à + le → au   à + les → aux
de + le → du   de + les → des

Exception: **l'** does not change or form a contraction:
| **Je vais à l'hôtel.** | I'm going to the hotel. |
| **Je viens de l'hôtel.** | I'm coming from the hotel. |

Partitive Articles and Amounts

If you wish to indicate an indefinite amount of something, you must use the so-called partitive articles. These are formed by using the preposition **de** together with the definite article.

Singular		Plural	
♂	♀	♂	♀
du pain	**de la bière**	**des jours**	**des pommes**
(some) bread	(some) beer	days	apples

On the other hand, if you wish to denote a definite amount, you must couple the nouns with **de**. **Beaucoup** (many/a lot of) and **peu** (few) also count as a "definite amount."

Singular		Plural	
♂	♀	♂	♀
une bouteille de lait	**un litre d'eau**	**un kilo d'abricots**	**un kilo de pommes**
a bottle of milk	a liter of water	a kilo of apricots	a kilo of apples

NOUNS

The Cases

The nominative and dative cases are identical in form. The genitive is formed with the help of the preposition **de**, the dative case with the propositon **à**.

Nominative	**Où est la gare?** Where is the station?
Genitive	**Où est la maison de ton oncle?** Where is your uncle's house?
Dative	**Je montre mon billet au contrôleur.** I show the inspector my ticket.
Accusative	**Je cherche la rue Mouffetard.** I'm looking for the Rue Mouffetard.

Plurals

1. As in English, the plural is almost always formed by the addition of an **-s**; however, this **-s** remains silent.
2. Words ending in **-al** usually form the plural using **-aux**.
   le journal – the newspaper → **les journaux**
3. One important irregular plural is **l'oeil** – the eye → **les yeux**. Note the pronounciation of the plural of **l'œuf** [lāf] – the egg → **les œufs** [lāzā].

ADJECTIVES AND ADVERBS

Adjectives

Adjectives conform to the nouns they modify in both gender and number.

An adjective is usually put into the feminine by adding an **-e** to the end of the masculine form. Some adjectives change slightly to accommodate this: the last consonant may be doubled, for example **-el → -elle (officiel → officielle)** or an accent mark will be added to the last vowel, for example **-ier → -ière (premier → première)**. These changes are also noteworthy: **-eux** and **-eur →** **-euse, -if → -ive, -eau → -elle**. If the masculine form already ends in an **-e**, then the adjective remains unchanged in the feminine. As with the nouns, the plural is generally made by adding an **-s** to the singular form.

Singular		Plural	
♂	♀	♂	♀
Le parc est grand.	**La ville est grande.**	**Les parcs sont grands.**	**Les villes sont grandes.**
The park is large.	The town is big.	The parks are large.	The towns are big.

Adjectives are usually placed after the noun:

un film intéressant an interesting film
la veste verte the green jacket

Short adjectives are generally placed before the noun. These include **bon** (good), **beau** (handsome/beautiful), **joli** (pretty), **jeune** (young), **vieux** (old), **grand** (large), and **petit** (small):

un bon repas   a good meal

Adverbs

Adverbs are formed by adding **-ment** to the end of the female adjective form:

froid – cold → **froide** → **froidement** – coldly.

There are also adverbs that do not derive from the adjective form; the most important ones are:

bien – well, **mal** – badly, **vite** – fast, **beaucoup** – much.

Comparatives

Adjectives and adverbs are intensified for the comparative by putting the word **plus** in front of them; the superlative is formed by using the comparative with a definite article:

grand	→	**plus grand (que)**	→	**le plus grand**
large		larger (than)		the largest
beau	→	**plus beau (que)**	→	**le plus beau**
handsome		handsomer (than)		the handsomest

Nicolas est plus beau que Lucas.
Nicolas is handsomer than Lucas.
Paris est la plus belle ville du monde.
Paris is the most beautiful city in the world.

PRONOUNS

Personal Pronouns

1. normal

	Nominative		Indirect Object		Direct Object	
Singular	**je**	I	**me**	(to) me	**me**	me
	tu	you	**te**	(to) you	**te**	you
	il	he	**lui**	(to) him	**le**	him/it
	elle	she		(to) her	**la**	her
Plural	**nous**	we	**nous**	(to) us	**nous**	us
	vous	you	**vous**	(to) us	**vous**	you
	ils	they ♂	**leur**	(to) them	**les**	them
	elles	they ♀				

On is often used instead of **nous** in casual speech: **On y va?** – Shall we go?

2. emphasized

Singular		Plural	
moi	I	**nous**	we
toi	you	**vous**	you
lui	he	**eux**	they ♂
elle	she	**elles**	they ♀

The emphasized forms are used as follows:

1. When they stand by themselves: **mon frère et moi** – my brother and I.
2. After prepositions: **sans toi** – without you.
3. To emphasize someone or something: **Lui, il est déjà parti.** – *He* is already gone.

Reflexive Pronouns

	Direct and Indirect Object	
Singular	**me**	myself
	te	yourself
	se	oneself
Plural	**nous**	ourselves
	vous	yourselves
	se	oneselves

In the French language, many actions refer back to the subject of the action in the form of reflexive verbs: **Je me lave les mains.** – I am washing my hands. **Nous nous levons à 8 heures.** – We get up at 8 o'clock.

Y and en

Y and **en** can replace the names of locations used with **à** and **de**, respectively:

Il va à Paris?	Is he going to Paris?
Oui, il y va.	Yes, he's going there.
Tu es à Tours?	Are you in Tours?
Oui, j'y suis.	Yes, I'm there.
Je viens de Paris.	I come from Paris.
J'en viens.	I come from there.

Y and **en** can also replace phrases beginning with **à** and **de**:

Tu pense à faire la vaisselle?	Will you remember to do the dishes?
J'y pense.	I'll remember to do it.
Il a mangé de la tarte?	Did he eat some of the tart?
Oui, il en a mangé.	Yes, he ate some of it.

Pronoun Placement

Pronouns are placed before the verb in this order:

me			
te	le		
se	la	lui	
nous	les	leur	y, en
vous			

245

For example:

Je vous le rends.	I give it back to you.
Je lui en parle.	I speak to him about it.

Possessive Pronouns

'Possession'	Singular				Plural
'Possessor'	♂		♀		♂ and ♀
Singular	**mon**		**ma**		**mes**
	ton	**fils**	**ta**	**fille**	**tes**
	son		**sa**		**ses**
					enfants
Plural	**notre**				**nos**
	votre	**fils, fille**			**vos**
	leur				**leurs**

The gender of the possessive pronoun always agrees with what is
referred to as belonging to the subject of the sentence and not
with the subject itself: **son fils** – his/her son, **sa fille** – his/her
daughter.

In these examples it is not clear whether the parent in question is
the mother or the father.

Note: Words that begin with a vowel or with the silent **h** always
take the masculine personal pronouns **mon**, **ton** and **son**: **mon
amie** – my (female) friend, **son histoire** – his/her story.

Demonstrative Pronouns

Singular		Plural	
♂	♀	♂	♀
ce pain this bread	**cette pomme** this apple	**ces pains** these breads	**ces pommes** these apples

Note: masculine words that begin with a vowel or the silent **h** use the demonstrative pronoun **cet**: **cet ami** – this friend, **cet hôtel** – this hotel.

The word for "that" and "it" in French is **cela**; it is often contracted to **ça**:

Cela/Ça me plaît.   I like it/that.

When placed before **être** (to be), **ce** means "that" or "it" (singular) or "they" or "those" (plural):

c'est ...   that/it is ...
ce sont ...   they/those are ...

Relative Pronouns

qui (nominative): **Je prends le train qui part à 8 heures.** – I'm taking the train that leaves at 8 o'clock.
que (accusative): **C'est l'homme que j'ai vu.** – That's the man that I saw.

VERBS

The most important tenses are:

The Present Tense: It expresses actions and situations taking place in the present: **Nicolas regarde son père.** – Nicolas is looking at his father.

The Future Tense: It expresses actions and situations in the future: **Demain, nous partirons en vacances.** – Tomorrow we are going on vacation.

You can put a verb in the future by using the infinitive (minus the final **-e**) and the proper ending: **donner + ai → donnerai**; **mettr(e) + ai → mettrai**. You can also express the future by using the present tense of **aller** (to go) with the infinitive: **Demain, nous allons partir en vacances.** – Tomorrow we are going to go on vacation.

The Past Tense: It expresses a situation or a repeated action in the past. It is formed by taking the root of the first person plural in the present tense and the proper ending: **finiss(ons) + ais → finissais.**

The Perfect Tense: It expresses a single, short-lived and/or sudden action in the past: **Nicolas lisait; tout à coup, le téléphone a sonné.** – Nicolas was reading; suddenly the phone rang. The perfect is usually formed by adding the past participle to the present of **avoir**: **j'ai + montré → j'ai montré.**
Reflexive verbs and action verbs, however, form the perfect with **être** instead of **avoir**: **Je suis allé au cinéma.** – I went to the movie theater.

248

You will frequently encounter the use of the Conditional: It expresses possibility and is often used in polite questions and - responses: **Vous pourriez me montrer ce livre?** – Could you show me this book? You will also need the conditional to make "ifthen" sentences: **Si j'avais assez d'argent, je t'en donnerais.** – If I had enough money I would give you some. As with the future tense, you can put a verb in the conditional by using the infinitive (minus the final **-e**) and adding the appropriate ending: **donner + ais → donnerais**.

Regular Verbs

In French verbs are classified by their infinitive endings:

1. Verbs ending in **-er**
2. Verbs ending in **-ir**
3. Verbs ending in **-re**

Most verbs belong to the first group.

	-er	-ir	-re
Infinitive	**donner** give	**finir** finish	**mettre** put
Present Tense	**je donne**	**je finis**	**je mets**
	tu donnes	**tu finis**	**tu mets**
	il donne	**il finit**	**il met**
	nous donnons	**nous finissons**	**nous mettons**
	vous donnez	**vous finissez**	**vous mettez**
	ils donnent	**ils finissent**	**ils mettent**

	-er	-ir	-re
Future	je donner*ai*	je finir*ai*	je mettr*ai*
Tense	tu donner*as*	tu finir*as*	tu mettr*as*
	il donner*a*	il finir*a*	il mettr*a*
	nous donner*ons*	nous finir*ons*	nous mettr*ons*
	vous donner*ez*	vous finir*ez*	vous mettr*ez*
	ils donner*ont*	ils finir*ont*	ils mettr*ont*
Past	je donn*ais*	je finiss*ais*	je mett*ais*
Tense	tu donn*ais*	tu finiss*ais*	tu mett*ais*
	il donn*ait*	il finiss*ait*	il mett*ait*
	nous donn*ions*	nous finiss*ions*	nous mett*ions*
	vous donn*iez*	vous finiss*iez*	vous mett*iez*
	ils donn*aient*	ils finiss*aient*	ils mett*aient*
Perfect	j'ai donn*é*	j'ai fin*i*	j'ai mis*
Tense	tu as donn*é*	tu as fin*i*	tu as mis
	il a donn*é*	il a fin*i*	il a mis
	nous avons donn*é*	nous avons fin*i*	nous avons mis
	vous avez donn*é*	vous avez fin*i*	vous avez mis
	ils ont donn*é*	ils ont fin*i*	ils ont mis
Condi-	je donner*ais*	je finir*ais*	je mettr*ais*
tional	tu donner*ais*	tu finir*ais*	tu mettr*ais*
	il donner*ait*	il finir*ait*	il mettr*ait*
	nous donner*ions*	nous finir*ions*	nous mettr*ions*
	vous donner*iez*	vous finir*iez*	vous mettr*iez*
	ils donner*aient*	ils finir*aient*	ils mettr*aient*

*mettre: irregular past participle: mis.

1   HUMAN RELATIONS

avoir and _être_

	avoir have	**être** be
Present Tense	j'ai tu as il a nous avons vous avez ils ont	je suis tu es il est nous sommes vous êtes ils sont
Future Tense	j'aurai tu auras il aura nous aurons vous aurez ils auront	je serai tu seras il sera nous serons vous serez ils seront
Past Tense	j'avais tu avais il avait nous avions vous aviez ils avaient	j'étais tu étais il était nous étions vous étiez ils étaient
Perfect Tense	j'ai eu tu as eu il a eu nous avons eu vous avez eu ils ont eu	j'ai été tu as été il a été vous avez été vous avez été ils ont été

	avoir have	**être** be
Conditional	**j'aurais**	**je serais**
	tu aurais	**tu serais**
	il aurait	**il serait**
	nous aurions	**nous serions**
	vous auriez	**vous seriez**
	ils auraient	**ils seraient**

Irregular Verbs

Here are the most frequently used irregular verbs conjugated in the present tense together with their further irregular forms:

aller go

Present Tense:	**je vais, tu vas, il va, nous allons, vous allez, ils vont**
Future Tense:	**j'irai, tu iras** etc.
Perfect Tense:	**je suis allé, tu es allé** etc.
Conditional:	**j'irais, tu irais** etc.

boire drink

Present Tense:	**je bois, tu bois, il boit, nous buvons, vous buvez, ils boivent**
Perfect Tense:	**j'ai bu, tu as bu** etc.
Conditional:	**je boirais, tu boirais** etc.

devoir have to

| Present Tense: | **je dois, tu dois, il doit, nous devons, vous devez, ils doivent** |
| Future Tense: | **je devrai, tu devras** etc. |

| Perfect Tense: | **j'ai dû, tu as dû** etc. |
| Conditional: | **je devrais, tu devrais** etc. |

faire do

Present Tense:	**je fais, tu fais, il fait, nous faisons, vous faites, ils font**
Future Tense:	**je ferai, tu feras** etc.
Perfect Tense:	**j'ai fait, tu as fait** etc.
Conditional:	**je ferais, tu ferais** etc.

pouvoir can

Present Tense:	**je peux, tu peux, il peut, nous pouvons, vous pouvez, ils peuvent**
Future Tense:	**je pourrai, tu pourras** etc.
Perfect Tense:	**j'ai pu, tu as pu** etc.
Conditional:	**je pourrais, tu pourrais** etc.

prendre take

Present Tense:	**je prends, tu prends, il prend, nous prenons, vous prenez, ils prennent**
Perfect Tense:	**j'ai pris, tu as pris** etc.
Conditional:	**je prendrais, tu prendrais** etc.

savoir know

Present Tense:	**je sais, tu sais, il sait, nous savons, vous savez, ils savent**
Future Tense:	**je saurai, tu sauras** etc.
Perfect Tense:	**j'ai su, tu as su** etc.
Conditional:	**je saurais, tu saurais** etc.

venir come

Present Tense:	**je viens, tu viens, il vient, nous venons, vous venez, ils viennent**
Future Tense:	**je viendrai, tu viendras** etc.
Perfect Tense:	**je suis venu, tu es venu** etc.
Conditional:	**je viendrais, tu viendrais** etc.

vouloir want to

Present Tense:	**je veux, tu veux, il veut, nous voulons, vous voulez, ils veulent**
Future Tense:	**je voudrai, tu voudras** etc.
Conditional:	**je voudrais, tu voudrais** etc.

NEGATIVE SENTENCES

The negative is expressed by using the word **ne** together with another word such as **pas**, **plus**, etc. These words surround the verb. In casual speech, however, the **ne** is often left out, so that the subsequent words **pas**, **plus**, etc. express the negation.

1. not: **ne ... pas**
   Ce n'est pas ma valise. That is not my suitcase.

2. nothing/not anything: **ne ... rien**
   Il n'a rien à manger. He has nothing to eat./He doesn't have anything to eat.

3. no more/not any more: **ne ... plus**
   Il n'y a plus d'essence. There's no more gas./There isn't any more gas.

4. nobody/not anybody: **ne ... personne**
   Je n'y ai vu personne.   I saw nobody there./I didn't see anybody there.

5. never: **ne ... jamais**
   Il ne fait jamais la vaisselle.   He never washes the dishes.

INTERROGATIVE SENTENCES

How to ask questions:

There are generally three ways to form interrogative sentences:

1. Using the word **est-ce que**:
   Est-ce que tu es contente?   Are you happy?

2. Transposing the subject and verb:
   Es-tu contente?   Are you happy?

3. Using rising inflection at the end of the sentence:
   Tu es contente?   Are you happy?

Interrogative Pronouns

The most important interrogative pronouns are:

when	**quand**	**Quand est-ce qu'il arrive?** When does he arrive?
why	**pourquoi**	**Pourquoi est-ce qu'elle ne vient pas?** Why doesn't she come?

what	qu'est-ce qui	Qu'est-ce qui se passe? What has happened?
	qu'est-ce que	Qu'est-ce que nous faisons demain? What are we going to do tomorrow?
which	quel, f: quelle	Quelle salade prendrez-vous? Which salad are you taking?
who(m)	a qui	À qui vous avez donné vos clés? Who(m) did you give your keys?
who(m)	qui	Qui voulez-vous voir? Who(m) would you like to see?
who	qui	Qui vient avec nous? Who is coming with us?
how	comment	Comment vas-tu? How are you?
how long	combien de temps	Combien de temps dure le voyage? How long does the journey take?
how much	combien	Combien coûte le billet? How much is the ticket?
where	où	Où sont les toilettes? Where are the rest rooms?
what ... of	à quoi	À quoi penses-tu? What are you thinking of?
what ... about	de quoi	De quoi parlez-vous? What are you talking about?
who(m) ... about	de qui	De qui parlez-vous? Who(m) are you talking about?

NUMBERS

Cardinal Numbers

0	zéro	zārō
1	un	eN
2	deux	dā
3	trois	trô·ä
4	quatre	kät'rə
5	cinq	seNk
6	six	sēs
7	sept	set
8	huit	ē·ēt
9	neuf	nāf
10	dix	dēs
11	onze	ôNz
12	douze	dōōz
13	treize	trez
14	quatorze	kätôrz
15	quinze	keNz
16	seize	sez
17	dix-sept	dēset
18	dix-huit	dēzē·ēt
19	dix-neuf	dēznāf
20	vingt	veN
21	vingt et un	veNtā·eN
22	vingt-deux	veNt-dā
23	vingt-trois	veNt-trô·ä
24	vingt-quatre	veNt-kät'rə
25	vingt-cinq	veNt-seNk

	vingt-six	veNt-sēs
	vingt-sept	veNt-set
	vingt-huit	veNtē̱-ēt
	vingt-neuf	veNt-nā̲f
	trente	träNt
	quarante	käräNt
	cinquante	seNkäNt
	soixante	sô-äsäNt
	soixante-dix	sô-äsäNtdēs
	quatre-vingts	kätrəveN
	quatre-vingt-dix	kätrəveNdēs
	cent	säN
	cent un	säN eN
	cinq cent soixante-dix-neuf	seNk säN sô-äsänt-dēs-nā̲f
	mille	mēl
	deux mille	dȧ̲ mēl
10 000	dix mille	dēs mēl

Ordinal Numbers

1st	premier	prəmyā
2nd	deuxième	dȧ̲zyem
3rd	troisième	trô-äzyem
4th	quatrième	kätrēyem
5th	cinquième	seNkyem
6th	sixième	sēsyem
7th	septième	setyem
8th	huitième	ē̱-ētyem
9th	neuvième	nā̲fyem